Becoming
A Young Woman
Who Pleases God

Pat
Ennis

NEW HOPE
PUBLISHERS
Birmingham, Alabama

New Hope® Publishers
P. O. Box 12065
Birmingham, AL 35202-2065
www.newhopepublishers.com
New Hope Publishers is a division of WMU®.

Library of Congress Cataloging-in-Publication Data

Ennis, Pat.
  Becoming a young woman who pleases God / Patricia Ennis.
      p. cm.
  Includes bibliographical references and index.
  ISBN-13: 978-1-59669-240-4 (sc : alk. paper)
  ISBN-10: 1-59669-240-5
  1. Teenage girls--Religious life. 2. Christian life--Biblical teaching. I. Title.
  BV4551.3.E55 2010
  248.8'33--dc22
                                    2010016233

ISBN-10: 1-59669-240-5
ISBN-13: 978-1-59669-240-4

N094136• 0910 • 3M1

I, Sarah Joy Abramson, invite you to read my personal notebook. It's morphed into a scrapbook of my senior year, including mementoes, sample assignments, lecture notes, small-group notes, doodles, notes from my parents, and more stuff. This records my triumphs, challenges, and how I made progress in becoming a young woman who pleases God. Walk with me and see how I...

I Dare You

The incredible search for a biblical worldview— what an adventure! Today, ideas are changing and there are many points of view on what's right and what's wrong.

- took the "The Incredible Adventure" (FYI)
- accepted character as more important than reputation (411)
- learned how to be a trustworthy friend (BFF)
- dared to nourish my body (MSG BOD)
- found out more about managing my money (L8$)
- discovered how to manage my time and avoid crises (IDK)
- started developing my worldview (I Serve U?)
- balanced modesty and wearing trends (TBD).
- learned how to tame my talk (TTYL).
- practiced biblical hospitality (TLC)
- began to understand God's special instructions to women (WORD).
- gained rewards because of choices I made in my senior year (by God's grace).
- learned tips on using a personal journal (CHAT).

Do you realize that surfing the Internet gives you a gazillion different views on morals and character, family, relationships, friends, body image, money, style, beliefs, and more? Which views are right for a young Christian woman, who wants to please God?

My small-group leader, Bethany, and Pastor John asked me, "What's a biblical worldview?"

I dare you to check out what I discovered! Look through my papers in this notebook and come up with your own findings, for your life.

I've recorded some of what I've been searching for as well as new discoveries. You'll find notes I took during all-school assembly, Senior Class group, small group, and Sunday services. I've doodled notes to my best friend on copies of some class assignments, lecture notes, and more.

I have a new phone I've used to pseudo-text my friends and my parents. So I used text for my notebook dividers. And I have a favorite pen my parents gave me to record my discoveries, especially the benefits I receive from my heavenly Father (sometimes I use hF. for short) and my prayers. I've journaled some of those here. Even on challenging days, I can praise God for who He is and the plans and purposes He has for me. The first words I'm writing are from His Word (HW). (I'm trying to memorize these two passages.)

"Bless the LORD, O my soul, and all that is within me, bless His holy name. Bless the LORD, O my soul, and forget none of His benefits; who pardons all your iniquities, who heals all your diseases; who redeems your life from the pit; who crowns you with lovingkindness and compassion; who satisfies your years with good things, so that your youth is renewed like the eagle" (Psalm 103:1–5). "For I am confident of this very thing, that He who began a good work in you will perfect it until the day of Christ Jesus" (Philippians 1:6).

My Prayer

Dear heavenly Father, please give me Your strength to always look for the ways You bless me. Help me believe—since I'm Your child—You'll continue the good work You started in me when I became Your daughter. Thank You that Your Word reminds me of that special day (Romans 3:10, 23; 5:8, 12; 6:23; 10:9-11, 13; 2 Corinthians 5:17). I love You, hF. Please help me to see how to bring glory to You this year. In Your name I pray, amen.

Your Prayer

(Here's a little space for you to write your own prayer to God as you look forward to all He wants to do to give you an incredible life; ask Him to help you read between the lines, see yourself as He sees you, and to help you understand the best of plans He has for your life.)

This senior notebook belongs to:

Sarah Joy Abramson
West Ranch High School
Class Officer: Service Club President

Parents: Zach and Liz

Nickname: Princess

Dad's occupation: pastor, New Hope Community Church

Mom: Homemaker and teacher, published author

Siblings: None

Principal: Mr. Solomon

Youth Pastor: Pastor John

Small-group leader: Bethany

BFF: Rebekah (Bekka)

Favorite Scripture: Proverbs 31

Emergency Contact ____Mom____

Schedule
Class	Semester Block	Instructor	Student ID
Humanities/English			
Health/P.E.			
Economics			
Sociology			
Work-Study			

Activities:
Campus Leadership
Club Service
Senior Group 168
Small-Group BS

What's in here:

This is packed with practical, biblical tools any young woman can use! I highly recommend for individual and group study, as well as homeschoolers.
— Program Director Ms. Eddie Baiseri, KBJS 90.3 FM, Jacksonville, TX

Cuts through confusion regarding young women's character...a precious tool to study Scriptures on their issues...thrilling challenge to spiritual maturity and excellence. We encourage you to drink deeply from this—your search will produce transformation in becoming a young woman who pleases God.
—Pastor Scott and Patty Ardavanis, Placerita Baptist Church, Newhall, California

FYI Adventure

(for you, incredible adventure)

Sunday MSG: A No Regret Year

Sunday afternoon, Pastor John planned a special event for the members of the high school group who are graduating this year. It was a great time of reflecting on the lessons we've learned about a godly lifestyle. He reminded us that as Christians we're to:

• Hunger and thirst after God (Psalm 42:1-2a).

• Have an attitude of submission to God's will and ways (James 4:7).

• Always choose to make biblical principles the first priority in our lives (Matthew 6:33).

• He then asked us to think about the legacy we're leaving to the younger students. What will they remember about us? Can we say with the Apostle Paul, "Follow me as we follow Christ" (1 Corinthians 11:1)? The challenge he laid before us was so awesome! Basically, throughout my senior year, I'm to:

• Believe God is sovereign regardless of what happens (Romans 8:28-29).

• Practice endurance and encouragement (Romans 15:5-6).

• Believe nothing is impossible (Philippians 4:13) and there is no good thing He will withhold from me if I'm walking out my faith (Psalm 84:11).

• Remember that since I only have one senior year, I should make up my mind and heart to enjoy every minute of it (Psalm 90:12).

• I know the Four Rs that concluded our time together will motivate me throughout my senior year:

• Give up my personal RIGHTS (1 Corinthians 13:4-8).

• Live so there'll be no REGRETS (Philippians 3:13-14; Hebrews 12:1-2; 2 Timothy 4:7-8).

• REJOICE instead of complaining (Philippians 4:4-8).

• Anticipate the REWARD (Hebrews 10:35-39).

Gracious heavenly Father, I really want this year to count for You. Please help me to live in such a way that my classmates will see You in me. And when the year comes to a conclusion, I pray I'll have no regrets. Knowing I can't do this in my own strength, I ask that You'll guide me each step of the way, for I know I can do all things when You strengthen me. I love You! Your daughter, Sarah.

168

Tonight was the first session of small group Bible studies for high school students. I chose the one led by Bethany, a student majoring in Home Economics-Family and Consumer Science at The Master's College. She announced the Scripture topic for this year: "The Incredible Adventure, The Quest for Becoming a Young Woman Who Pleases God."

She began by saying that Proverbs 31:10-31 introduces a woman whose lifestyle, values, and character match up with the Word of God. This passage, according to Bethany, paints a word portrait of a woman whose life challenges twenty-first century Christian young women to follow. She also shared that the immutability (changelessness) of God is in question if we don't believe Proverbs 31:10-31 is practical for us today. In other words, we don't wait until we have gray hair and a cane to begin applying the verses.

When she suggested the description of the godly woman of Proverbs 31:10-31 isn't designed to give women an inferiority complex, I thought, guys don't have 21 consecutive verses that make them feel inadequate. But then, she explained the passage gives a biblical basis for developing principles that have priorities for a young woman who desires to be considered a woman who pleases God. In fact, 11 principles inspire the young woman seeking to please God. She is virtuous, trustworthy, energetic, physically fit, economical, unselfish, honorable, lovable, prepared, prudent, and God-fearing, just as a book called, <u>Becoming a Woman Who Pleases God</u> teaches.

"Are you willing to begin the incredible search?"

Virtuous (31:10) is an inner quality that instinctively demands respect. Moral excellence characterizes the WTIP's behavior (Ruth 3:11).

Trustworthy (31:11-12) is the ability to keep another's confidence. A godly young woman's speech is encouraging, sympathetic, and tactful (Proverbs 25:11). Her love of her Lord is evident (John 14:15), and dependability is exhibited in her lifestyle (Proverbs 25:23).

Energetic (31:13-16, 19, 24, 27) suggests that a godly young woman works hard instead of looking for the easy way to complete a responsibility (Proverbs 10:4). Her Christianity is practical (James 1:17). She enjoys her work (John 4:36) and attacks it with a cheery attitude (Colossians 3:17).

Physically Fit (31:17) reminds us that to perform our duties efficiently we must be healthy. Young women who want to please God seek to understand their bodies and then work within their strengths and weaknesses (1 Corinthians 6:19).

Economical (31:18) means we're good managers of every resource we have—time, money, and so on. This also means we're content with what God gives us rather than always wanting more (1 Timothy 6:6-8).

Unselfish (31:18) is displayed in our willingness to share our most valuable asset—our time—with others. A WTIP isn't so busy with her own activities that she can't lend a helping hand to others. Her words bring comfort, hope, cheer, and, when necessary, correction to those who touch her life (Galatians 6:10).

Honorable (31:25) is reflected in her choice to "stay away from every form of evil"
(1 Thessalonians 5:22). She dresses trendy, but modestly, and understands the importance of maintaining the character quality of integrity (Proverbs 22:1, 31:22).

Lovable (31:28-29) is seen in the consistency of her lifestyle. She enjoys relationships that have depth because she seeks to sharpen her friends spiritually and intellectually (Proverbs 27:17). Because she is lovable, she is fun to be with (John 10:10).

Prepared (31:21-22) allows a WTIP to cope confidently with unforeseen circumstances (Philippians 4:13).

Prudent (31:26) means a wise young woman is careful of consequences; she considers her decisions' long-term effects. When she speaks, she is kind yet firm (Proverbs 27:9b).

God-fearing (31:30) means her actions and lifestyle consistently reflect respect for her Lord (Proverbs 1:7) and she loves Him with all her heart (Matthew 22:37).

Proverbs 31:31 describes the reward of developing the 11 principles. It tells us a WTIP receives her rewards "in the gates," (Proverbs 31:23)—in public. She is often rewarded in this life and always in the hereafter (1 Corinthians 3:10-15; 4:1-51; 1 Corinthians 5:10; Revelation 22:12).

Bethany

Practical suggestions to make principles apply in real life.

- Daily build spiritual stamina: when hard times come, face them with peace and confidence rather than fear or anxiety (Psalm 119:11).
- Choose to <u>wear</u> humility. Like a garment, it's flowing design allows you freedom to serve others graciously (1 Peter 5:5-6).
- Intentionally give cares and concerns to God. He alone is able to fix them (Psalm 55:22, 1 Peter 5:8).
- Select words carefully. Never be sorry for things spoken or unspoken (Proverbs 31:26).
- Consistently show love to others—even when you don't feel like it. Remember that love is never impolite (1 Corinthians 13:5).
- Be countercultural! Twenty-first century society urges young women to assert and stand up for their rights. But focus on the truth: becoming a WTIP is a sign of strength rather than weakness (1 Peter 2:18-25).
- Enjoy every day of life. WTIPs who please God are peaceful, calm, and joyful—even when circumstances are difficult (John 10:10).
- Believe you can become a young woman who pleases God through the Lord's strength (Philippians 4:13).

As I finish this journal entry tonight, I'm answering Bethany's question as prayer to my loving hF! Dear God, I truly want to be a young woman who pleases You. I pray that as I live this year You'll create a desire in me to honestly make these 11 principles part of my life. In Your name I pray, amen.

? 4 U

I'll share some of my thoughts with you but you can write answers in the margins and spaces here, or even in your journal or scrapbook.

How can I live so I have no regrets at the end of each day (Philippians 4:13)?

What verses of Scripture will help me focus on having a "no regret day" (like Psalm 119:11)?

I commit to thank my hF daily for the strength He provides me to experience a "no regret day" (1 Thessalonians 5:16-18. (It's always helpful to journal prayers.)

When necessary, I can ask my heavenly Father to forgive me if I don't experience a "no regret day" (1 John 1:9).

(My start for chart of personal goals for the WTIP principles. I've expanded in following tabs.).

(Name here) _____, WTIP

PRINCIPLE AND PERSONAL DEFINITION	VERSE	PERSONAL GOALS
Virtuous Practically wise and careful of the consequences	Proverbs 31:30	1. Place everything read, viewed, or listened to through the grid of Philippians 4:8-9.

How does the principle of virtuous apply to what's in this notebook so far?

Practical ways to apply the principle of virtuous to my life are: I will pray my heavenly Father will motivate me to put the items on the list into action.

Studying the life of Ruth, the only woman in the Bible described as a "virtuous woman," I've discovered these examples of how she:
Supported and loved a bitter mother-in-law.
Worked hard to provide for herself and Naomi.
Listened to Naomi's advice.

More:

First all-school assembly, Principal Solomon announced writing contest for school year: "It's What's Inside That Counts." It's his hope we'll be more concerned about our character (who we are inside) than how we look or what we have. He also said, at the end of the school year, an award will be presented to a freshman, sophomore, junior, and senior who have best exemplified the Six Pillars of Character throughout the year. I decided to write an essay on this, too, for my humanities class. Here are my notes from his presentation, followed by the essay.

Lecture Notes:
Character—What Is It?
The desire to encourage twenty-first-century society to embrace some form of ethical values has led to founding of many organizations. such as Josephson Institute. The sole purpose of the organization is to remind people "character does count." Their publication states a person of character: is a good person. someone to look up to and admire; knows the difference between right and wrong and always tries to do what is right; sets a good example for everyone; makes the world a better place; lives according to the Six Pillars of Character: trustworthiness. respect. responsibility. fairness. caring. and citizenship. Check out www.charactercounts.org for this and more information on how the program works and to help with essay.

Pillar One—Trustworthiness
· Be honest · Don't deceive, cheat or steal · Be reliable—do what you say you'll do · Have the courage to do the right thing · Build a good reputation · Be loyal—stand by your family, friends, and country.

Pillar Two—Respect
· Treat others with respect; follow the Golden Rule · Be tolerant of differences · Use good manners, not bad language · Be considerate of the feelings of others · Don't threaten, hit, or hurt anyone · Deal peacefully with anger, insults, and disagreements.

Pillar Three—Responsibility
· Do what you are supposed to do · Persevere: keep on trying! · Always do your best · Use self-control · Be self-disciplined · Think before you act—consider the consequences · Be accountable for your choices.

Pillar Four—Fairness
·Play by the rules · Take turns and share · Be open-minded; listen to others · Don't take advantage of others · Don't blame others carelessly.

Pillar Five—Caring
·Be kind · Be compassionate and show you care · Express gratitude · Forgive others · Help people in need.

Pillar Six—Citizenship
·Do your share to make your school and community better · Cooperate · Get involved in community affairs · Stay informed; vote · Be a good neighbor · Obey laws and rules · Respect authority · Protect the environment.

[The Six Pillars of Character, Josephson Institute]

These pillars are going to be integrated into West Ranch campus life this year. A color scheme will decorate halls and classrooms to remind us. Trustworthiness = Blue — think "true blue." Yellow/Gold = Respect — think the Golden Rule. Green = Responsibility — think being responsible for a garden or finances, or as in being solid and reliable like an oak. Orange = Fairness — think of dividing an orange into equal sections to share fairly with friends. Caring = Red — think of a heart. Citizenship = Purple — think regal purple as representing the state.
The acronym doesn't exactly spell terrific but it's close: Trustworthiness Respect Responsibility Fairness Caring Citizenship!

My mom made this amazing pot roast for dinner, and I talked to her and Dad before writing my essay: "How the Six Pillars of Character Fit with being a Christian."
Mom reminded me—reputation is what I'm supposed to be while character is what I am. If I'm only trying to fulfill the Six Pillars of Character to win the award or look good at school as a Christian,

that's not pleasing to God. She encouraged me to check out 1 Samuel 16:7. Its words, "for the LORD sees not as man sees: man looks on the outward appearance, but the LORD looks on the heart" (ESV) challenged me to make sure I'm truly working on developing godly character all year.

Dad zeroed in on how following the pillars fits with being a Christian. He reminded me the Word of God is my standard for behavior; not the "Six Pillars." I'm to be a Christian first and a student at West Ranch High second. God's Word challenges me to cultivate a lifestyle that conforms me to the image of Jesus Christ, the only person who exhibited character in its purest form. He encouraged me to study the Six Pillars of Character with the Bible to see if I can find scriptural support. If so, it's good for me to attempt to follow them. If not, then I'm to follow the higher standard, the Bible. It took me a while but here's what I found: This study is a discovery of what it means to me to have character—godly character—and is part of my biblical worldview.

Pillar	Bible Reference	Behavior to Practice
1-Trustworthiness		
• Be honest.	• Romans 13:13-14	• Live a life that shows I'm a Christian.
• Don't deceive, cheat, or steal.	• Exodus 20:15	• Don't dishonestly take anything that belongs to someone else.
• Be reliable—do what you say you'll do.	• Matthew 21:28-32	• Remember the parable of the two sons—it's important to do what I say I will do.
• Have the courage to do the right thing.	• Acts 4:13-19, 5:22-29	• Follow Peter and John's example of boldness.
• Build a good reputation.	• Proverbs 22:1	• Live in such a way that others have no reason to question my character.
• Be loyal—stand by your family, friends, and country.	• Proverbs 17:17	• Choose to love at all times—even when it is hard.
2-Respect		
• Treat others with respect; follow the Golden Rule.	Matthew 7:12; Luke 6:31	• I'm to treat others the way I wish to be treated.
• Be tolerant of differences.	• James 2:1-4	• Don't show partiality.
• Use good manners, not bad language.	• Proverbs 11:16, 15:23	• Be gracious; speak encouraging words.

• Be considerate of the feelings of others.	• Hebrews 10:24	• Encourage others.
• Don't threaten, hit, or hurt anyone.	• Romans 12:17	• Have godly behavior around others, especially unbelievers.
• Deal peacefully with anger, insults and disagreements.	• Romans 12:18	• Do everything possible to be at peace with others.

3—Responsibility

• Do what you are supposed to do.	• Colossians 3:17	• I'm to not only do what I'm supposed to do; I'm to do it with a good attitude!
• Persevere: keep on trying!	• Philippians 3:12-14	• I'm to continue to pursue being Christ-like.
• Always do your best.	• 1 Corinthians 10:31	• Everything I do is to bring glory to God.
• Use self-control.	• Galatians 5:22-26	• Self-control is one of the fruits of the spirit. I show I'm a member of God's family by having self-control.
• Be self-disciplined.	• 2 Peter 1:5-6	• I'm to have the same self-discipline in my Christian life as athletes do in their sport.

· Think before you act—consider the consequences.	· Galatians 6:7	· I will reap the consequences of both the good and bad decisions that I make.
· Be accountable for your choices.	· James 5:16	· I'm to be accountable to other believers in the body of Christ.

4-Fairness

· Play by the rules.	· John 14:15	· I show I love God when I keep His commandments.
· Take turns and share.	· Philippians 2:1-4	· I'm to be careful to not push to always have things go my way.
· Be open-minded; listen to others.	· James 1:19	· I should know God's Word so I can compare what they say with God's opinion.
· Don't take advantage of others.	· 1 Corinthians 13:4	· I'm to practice biblical love and refuse to use others for my advantage.
· Don't blame others carelessly.	· 1 Corinthians 13:7	· I'm to believe the best about others.

5-Caring

·Be kind.	· Ephesians 4:32	· Treat others the same way Jesus would.

• Be compassionate and show you care.	• 1 Peter 3:8	• Look for ways to show concern for others.
• Express gratitude.	• 1 Thessalonians 5:18	• Remember that thanklessness is characteristic of unbelievers. Therefore, I should always express gratitude.
• Forgive others.	• Colossians 3:12-13	• Follow Christ's model of forgiveness. Since He forgave all my sins I must be willing to forgive others.
• Help people in need.	• James 2:14-16	• I must show my compassion for others' needs by being willing to physically help them. This is faith in action.

6-Citizenship

• Do your share to make your school and community better.	• Romans 13:2-7	• Since God designed human government I'm to submit to it whenever possible
• Cooperate.	• Titus 3:1-2	• Submit to authority.

· Get involved in community affairs.	· Matthew 5:14	· Exhibit godly behavior when participating in community affairs.
· Stay informed; vote.	· Matthew 5:13	· Be a savoring influence by knowing about current events and voting when I'm eligible.
· Be a good neighbor.	· James 2:8	· Be willing to meet the physical and spiritual needs of others.
· Obey laws and rules.	· Romans 13:1	· Obey laws and rules unless obedience would require disobedience to God's Word.
· Respect authority.	· 1 Peter 2:13	· Be an obedient citizen so my heavenly Father is glorified.
· Protect the environment.	· Genesis 1:28	· Take good care of God's creation.

My Prayer

HF, Your Word is clear about how I'm to behave. Your standards are higher than the Six Pillars. Help me each day to say to those whose lives I touch, "Be imitators of me, just as I also am of Christ" (I Corinthians 11:1). I know You look at my heart, so help me be more concerned about pleasing You than looking good to others. I know I can have genuine godly character throughout this year, only with Your strength in my life. In Jesus' name, amen.

SG 168

Tonight was the first senior high group meeting for the fall. 168 stands for number of hours in the week. The name reminds us to make the most of each day. Our Scripture is, "Every moment, every breath, every opportunity for the glory of God" (Ephesians 5:15-21).

Pastor John introduced our theme—Gauging Our Gratitude. Some of us groaned while others expressed with our faces our lack of enthusiasm. Many thought parents had something to do with it. We had to sit through this evenings presentation—listening or not.

He began by saying what we could all identify with: "Most of us complain far more than we should, and we don't realize what negative effects our complaining has on our spiritual lives." He then asked us to complete this sentence, "When a situation goes wrong, my normal reaction is to __." It was embarrassing for me to fill in the blank (glad I didn't have to respond out loud!). I had to admit that while I may smile, I often grumble and complain inwardly. I guess he read my mind because his next statement seemed just for me, "The best antidote for a complaining spirit is a grateful heart, and that heart must be allowed to develop every moment of every day. Giving thanks is a biblical instruction, not a suggestion, and cultivating a grateful heart is a life-long process."

The entire Book of Psalms is written to our wills, not our emotions, meaning we need do what will please our HF whether we feel like it or not. Then he asked a personal question, "What is your Gratitude Gauge?" The next few minutes, we were going to measure our gratitude. He had several of the guys pass out The Gratitude Gauge handout and asked us to move our chairs so we could fill it out without looking on each others' papers. It was a little noisy to begin with, but as we answered the questions the room became very quiet. I'm thankful to have a copy of it to keep and to share with others. What do you think?

The Gratitude Gauge

Write the number that best reflects your response to the statement in the space provided.

Scale:

5 = regularly

4 = usually

3 = sometimes

2 = seldom

1 = very seldom

0 = never

_____I'm quick to acknowledge that expressing gratitude is a biblical instruction.

_____I recognize a complaining spirit is symptomatic of lacking a grateful heart.

_____I understand cultivating a grateful heart is a life-long process.

_____I believe the condition of my spiritual heart determines my spiritual health.

_____I'm increasing in my knowledge of the Word.

_____I thank my heavenly Father for my spiritual blessings.

_____I thank my heavenly Father for my material blessings.

_____I thank my heavenly Father for my joyful experiences.

_____I thank my heavenly Father for my difficult experiences.

_____I offer thanks to others when they extend kindness to me.

_____I seek to speak encouraging words to others.

_____I'm quick to acknowledge that sincere gratitude enriches my life.

_____I'm seeking to serve others.

_____I maintain contact with missionaries and seek to share some of their burdens.

_____I understand that giving thanks is generated from my will.

_____I'm aware that being thankful is generated from my emotions.

_____I "pause for praise" throughout the day.

_____Others affirm my grateful spirit.

_____I acknowledge that how I respond to the biblical instruction about expressing gratitude affects my spiritual health.

_____I'm like the one leper described in Luke 17:15-16 who returned to thank the Lord for healing him.

_____Gratitude Gauge Total

(See The Gratitude Gauge Interpretation in *?4U on my page 30.*)

Mine wasn't as bad as it could be, but it wasn't great either. Before we closed in prayer Pastor John announced next week's topic—"The Value of Developing a Heart of Gratitude." I knew I needed to come even if no one else showed up!

My Prayer

Heavenly Father, I know I displease You when I complain, whether I do it orally or mentally. I have so many things to be thankful for. Please help me to have a grateful spirit instead of a complaining one—oh, and please help me to be excited about this year's senior high group's theme. In Your name I pray, amen.

168

Bible Study Notes. When I walked into the high school room this evening, I was surprised to find it full. It was exciting to know I wasn't the only one who needed to learn how to develop a heart of gratitude. After some great songs and announcements, Pastor John began his presentation by asking another question. "What is the heart?" Of course there were a bunch of silly responses before we settled down to the "heart" of the lesson.

Developing a Heart of Gratitude

Christians are to be concerned with two forms of the heart; the physical heart and the spiritual heart. The physical heart provides nourishment, sustenance, and energy throughout the entire body. If a weakness, either by breakdown or disease, occurs within the heart, it could lead to weaknesses in the rest of the body.

The spiritual heart is the center of thinking and reason (Proverbs 3:3, 6:21, 7:3), the emotions (Proverbs 15:15, 30), and the will (Proverbs 11:20; 14:14). It's the source of whatever affects our speech (Proverbs 4:24), sight (Proverbs 4:25), and conduct (Proverbs 4:26-27).

The condition of our spiritual heart determines our spiritual health and ultimately controls how we respond to the biblical instruction to develop a heart of gratitude. Proverbs teaches us we have either a wicked and foolish heart or a righteous and wise heart. The wicked and foolish heart despises correction (Proverbs 5:12), is proud (Proverbs 14:14, 18:2, 12), lacks good judgment (Proverbs 12:23, 19:3), and is hard (Proverbs 28:14). The righteous and wise heart is very different. It's teachable (receives commands) (Proverbs 10:8), has wisdom and understanding (Proverbs 14:33), seeks knowledge (Proverbs 15:14), and learns and grows (Proverbs 16:23).

Question: Which type of heart do you have?

Before you answer, pray God will give you the desire to have a heart that pleases Him. So many times, we find we have a wicked heart. We can ask, as the Psalmist David did, that God will create in us a clean heart and renew a devoted spirit within us.

When we possess a righteous and wise heart, we're quick to express gratitude. Gratitude is defined as the quality of being thankful and a readiness to show appreciation for and to return kindness. Christians daily experience God's kindness to them. However, we get so busy, we don't stop to think of all that God has done for us. Often we become like the child who, seeing the stack of birthday gifts, quickly unwraps them rather than enjoying each one and offering gratitude for it. We are so eager to get to the next thing on our schedule that we fail to stop, look, enjoy, and give thanks. We need to pause for praise throughout the day to thank God and others for the things done for us." The most important place to start is to thank God for forgiveness of sin. As we begin to praise the Lord for His goodness to us we find that giving thanks to others comes easily.

People who are outside of Christ are used to hearing complaining. They may not know what to do with somebody who joyfully praises the Lord as Paul did when he and Silas were in jail (Acts 16:25-34). The Philippian jailor wasn't brought to Christ by the earthquake—that made him want to commit suicide! It was because Paul and Silas praised the Lord, under difficult circumstances, that the man heard the gospel and learned that there was a way of salvation.

A complaining Christian is a pitiful witness; too much like the world to have much effect on the world. The senior high group is not an effective witness for our Lord because most of us neglect praise and thanksgiving. Complaining sometimes seems like the glue that bonds us together. It's the lifestyle of gratitude that provides convincing testimony of the saving power of God—and that brings glory to Him (Matthew 5:16; 1 Peter 2:11-12).

If we want a righteous and wise at heart, then we will practice gratitude. The story of the ten lepers is a reminder of the fact that we often accept blessing without saying "thank you."

Questions

Are you like the nine lepers who never returned to give thanks to the Lord Jesus or like the one who did (Luke 17:11-19)?

What is your response to the warning found in 2 Timothy 3:1-7?

What are some of the blessings Psalm 103 speaks about? "Bless the Lord, O my soul; and all that is within me, bless His holy name!" running through my mind (v1).

When considering it's what's inside that counts, my Health teacher covered some material that fits here. My favorite class! Today we started studying about hospitality. Our teacher, Mrs. T. is really cool. She knows a lot, and she lives it out. She started class with "one of the most important parts of hospitality is to show simple kindness" (that is a definition of manners) when we either invite others to be our guests or we have the privilege of being a guest. She also reminded us that having good manners is a part of Pillar Two—Respect.

Mrs. T broke our class into groups. She had us use our textbook as a resource to answer questions that would help us understand basic manners. Here is what we found, including using the book Becoming a Woman Who Pleases God, coauthored by Pat Ennis:

Do Manners Really Matter?

Invitations
- Respond to any invitation no later than the *RSVP (Repondez S'il Vous Plait*, which is French for "respond, please") to tell the hostess whether or not you plan to attend.
- It's not OK to bring others with you unless you first check with the hostess.
- Respect the host and hostess and show your interest in the event by being on time. Arrive no earlier than 15 minutes before the function begins, and no more than 15 minutes after the function begins.
- Younger people are introduced to older people, and people of all ages are introduced to people in authority. Teens shouldn't use first names unless invited to do so. Always give good eye contact during introductions.
- Give a hostess gift, a small item a guest takes when entertained in a person's home for a meal or overnight, to show appreciation for the kindness.

Important reminders for guests
- Cancel only in case of emergency.
- Don't "double book" and try to attend more than one occasion.
- Offer help to the hostess.
- Talk with the other guests.
- Don't attend if you're sick!
- Ask the hostess about dress; be modest.
- Don't be first or last to leave.
- Always tell your hostess you enjoyed yourself, before leaving.
- You can also email, text, or call your hostess the next day to say thanks.
- Send a thank-you note immediately.

What manners are important if I'm an overnight guest?
- Fit in or exceed the family's standard of orderliness.
- Keep your living area clean; make your bed, unless told not to or it's the day you're leaving.
- Unless you have a private bathroom, remove personal items after each use; keep the bathroom clean.
- Don't use the phone or computer without asking.
- Respect the hostess's house and all belongings.
- Fit your schedule to your host's and hostess's.

- Blend in with the family.
- Don't use all the hot water, listen to the television, or music too loudly, or ask for too many items you forgot.
- Offer to help.

How do I know what table manners to use?
- Follow your host's and hostess's example.
- Wait for the hostess to be seated before taking a seat.
- Allow the gentleman to seat the lady to his right. He pulls out her chair for her, and she waits for him to seat her. Once seated, he then takes his seat beside her.
- Watch the hostess when placing the napkin. She may place her napkin in her lap before the blessing or wait until after to do so. It may be unfolded or left folded in half with the fold against the body. The napkin is placed on the seat if you leave the table during the meal. At the end of the meal, It's placed to the right of the plate. It does not need to be refolded and should *not* be wadded up.
- Never place dirty silver on table linens.
- Watch the hostess to know which piece of silverware to use.

How should I act during the meal?
- Sit where the hostess tells you to sit.
- Taste your food before adding salt or pepper.
- When chewing, close your mouth.
- Don't make noise with your silverware.
- Sit up straight in your chair.
- Don't eat too slowly or quickly; match the other guests.
- Take a small serving of all foods.
- Be gracious in speech and action.
- Be polite and patient with other guests.
- Watch your hostess for cues.
- Plan to enjoy yourself!

As Mom and I chatted over an afternoon snack, I shared Mrs. T's project for the day and asked if the Bible says manners matter. As always, she thought before answering. And she put it in writing for my notebook.

From Mom.
Good manners are behaviors definitely missing in our twenty first-century Christian culture. A woman's manners, no matter what her age, are a mirror that show her true character. "For though I am free from all men, I have made myself a slave to all, so that I may win the more. I have become all things to all men, that I may by all means save some" (1 Corinthians 9:19-22). Christians often fail to practice good manners and that can affect their witness to the world.
"A gracious woman attains honor" (Proverbs 11:16), and "like a gold ring in a [pig's] snout so is a beautiful woman who lacks discretion [good judgment]" (Proverbs 11:22).

As we finished our snack, I cleared the table, gave her a big hug, and went to my room. Before starting homework, I knew I needed to journal this prayer.

HF, thank You for Mrs. T and my mom who are such wonderful examples of practicing good manners. Thank You that Psalm 145 describes Your character. Please help me practice good manners so I don't discredit my testimony for You. In Your name I pray, amen.

You can study each of the Scriptures in Six Pillars of Character with a chart of your own. You can complete— like this one.

? 4 U

Pillar	Bible Reference	What the Bible Reference Means to Me	Behavior to Practice

Complete The Gratitude Gauge too. Compare your score with the Interpretation. Journal a description of your results.

The Gratitude Gauge Interpretation

100-90—a maturing ❤ of gratitude

89-80—a commitment to a ❤ of gratitude

79-70—an understanding of what constitutes a ❤ of gratitude

69-60—a minimal commitment to a ❤ of gratitude

59-0—a ❤ transplant is needed

How does the principle of *energetic* apply to this chapter? Practical ways I can apply the principle of *energetic* to my life:

I pray my hF will motivate me to put the items on my list into action.

Studying the life of the Shunammite woman, who had a rich husband and could have spent her days in leisure, gives us answers to these questions:

What did she do with her extra time?

How did the Shunammite woman extend hospitality?

How can I follow her example and practice hospitality?

The Shunammite woman used her resources to serve God. How can I use what I have to serve Him?

What blessings did the Shunammite woman receive?

Recorded here are some of the blessings God has given me (Psalm 103 is one of my models):

BFF?

My heart's sad. Something's wrong with my friendship with Bekka. my
BFF. We've known each other since we were in New Hope's nursery
together! At the beginning of our senior year. we were excited to
share its joys and challenges together. Now it seems she doesn't
want to be friends—at least not best friends.
At first I thought it was my imagination. Today I realized it's not.
We always do something special together to celebrate our birthdays:
mine is today. She gave me a nice gift and card but said nothing
about hanging out together. Bekka's rejection made it difficult to
enjoy the many other kind things people did. I talked with my parents about what to do. They encouraged me to pray first and then
think about the friendship David and Jonathan shared. So I journaled
this prayer.

*Dear hF, you know my heart's sad 'cause of Bekka's rejection. It's hard to believe she
wouldn't want to celebrate my birthday with me. I know You know all about rejection. Please give me Your strength to continue to love her. And show me whether I've
done anything wrong to her. If I have, I want to ask her to forgive me, and restore
our friendship. Help me to be careful to follow my parents' advice and study what
Your Word says about friendship. In Your name I pray, amen.*

What Dad says. One of the best descriptions of friendship
recorded in Scripture is Jonathan and David's (1 Samuel 18:1-4.
19. 20-42; 23:16; 2 Samuel 1:17). He encouraged me to study some
of the qualities of their friendship and compare them with the
friendship Bekka and I share.
What I found. The first description in 1 Samuel 18 says friendship needs someone to take the initiative to get it started (18:1).
At church and school. it seems too many people base friendships
on surface stuff and selfishness. Genuine—that's what I see in
the start of Jonathan's friendship with David: willingness to cross
social barriers and selfish ambition to build friendship. Maybe one
of the problems with my friendship with Bekka is neither of us

really started the relationship. First, we were friends because our parents are friends.

I realized unselfishness is necessary to be a true friend (18:4; 23:16-17). Each person may need to give up something treasured. Jonathan willingly gave up his rightful position as king. I know with Bekka, sometimes we both want to be in control. I'm praying my hF will help me consider her wishes, even if it means she doesn't want to spend time with me.

Friendship looks out for the other person's best interests. Jonathan wanted to warn David of danger (19:1-2), defend him, and encourage Saul and David to make up (19:3-7). Jonathan's unselfish actions placed his safety and relationship with his dad in danger. Though I want to reconcile with Bekka, I must be unselfish. Maybe being friends with Bekka isn't best for her right now. Friends sacrifice to help each other (20:24-42). As Jonathan was willing to help David, I want to help Bekka.

HF, Your Word is clear about how I should treat others, even people who seem unkind to me. Help me follow Your example of loving my friends at all times. In Your name I pray, amen.

Turned-Head Weed

The Turned-Head Weed grows in one direction while its head faces the opposite. It might be called the "if only" weed because it lives on memories of other friendships and past experiences. It can ruin new friendships by always talking about other "better" friendships or by having unrealistic expectations of current ones. This weed is best removed by thanking God for precious memories built in other relationships and by then concentrating on building the new friendships He gives (Ephesians 5:20; Philippians 3:13; 1 Thessalonians 5:18).

Mom's advice.

Mom seems to always use some kind of metaphor when she explains stuff to me. Like, she says there are many "weeds that can get in the way of the growth of love in my friendship garden." I laughed when she explained some of them because her descriptions are so true of the way my friends and I sometimes treat each other. I really got serious when she reminded me that if I let any of the "weeds take root in my friendship garden," I'm sinning!

I-Me Weed

A fancy name for selfishness, the I-Me Weed grows to enormous heights until nothing else in the garden can be seen. It's a real love-choker, often turning friendships into thickets of fighting and competition. This weed creates an environment directly opposite of the kind of love commanded by God. This love, known as agape, challenges me to accept my friend exactly as she is. This means I forgive and forget unintended snubs or insults. I place no demands on the friendship and allow the will rather than the emotions to control it. (Mom reminded me that the entire Book of Psalms is written to the will, not the emotions. She encouraged me to read through the Psalms and underline every "I will" I find.). This weed quickly establishes itself as the center and demands to be in control. It's most effectively removed by sowing the Our-We seed in its place (Proverbs 13:10; Galatians 5:15; 19-25; Philippians 2:3; James 3:16).

Clam-Up Weed

The Clam-Up Weed is one of the most difficult to remove because when one friend "clams up" or stops communicating it's almost impossible to correct the situation. When this weed invades, the silence that falls over the friendship garden is like the silence of a tomb. The presence of this weed often leads to the suppression of one's feelings. Often suppression eventually erupts in an explosion.
To remove this weed it's important to talk frequently and honestly. The tone, choice, and number of your words should be carefully chosen. Should disagreements arise, I am to refuse to remain angry and be willing to admit my contribution to the conflict (Proverbs 25:11; 26:20; 31:26; Ephesians 4:15, 25-32).

Wandering Affection Weed

The Wandering Affection Weed is small, ugly, and has sharp leaves and roots that cut the roots of love under the surface, out of sight, so a friendship doesn't know what is happening until it's too late. This weed seeks to develop a new friendship by destroying an existing one. The Wandering Affection Weed whispers mean comments about existing friends, suggests that another friend can better fulfill my friendship needs, and hints it's OK to end a long-established friendship for a new one.
While it's a good choice to make new friends, it's not right to dump deeply rooted friendships to do so. Getting rid of the Wandering Affection Weed includes: refusing to damage the reputation of my friend (Ephesians 4:29; Colossians 3:8), choosing to "love at all times" (Proverbs 17:17), seeking to bear my friend's burdens (Galatians 6:2), often choosing what's pleasing to her (Hebrews 10:24), and focusing on her positive qualities rather than her weaknesses (Psalm 101:5; Proverbs 6:19; 17:17; Galatians 6:2, 10; Philippians 4:8-9).

I m Always Right Weed

Standing stiff and rigid in the friendship garden, the person possessing characteristics of the I Am Always Right Weed offers a sharp, unkind response to anything she disagrees with. Many ugly words can come from her lips if she is irritated. When she takes on this attitude, engaging in conversation with her is useless since she is always right.

Removal of this weed needs prayer on my part so the words of my mouth and the meditations of my heart are acceptable to the Lord (Psalm 19:14). Filling my mind with God's Word so my responses are His responses and being willing to graciously and gently speak the truth in love guarantee I am not providing ammunition to keep the conflict going. (See Psalms 19:14; 39:1; 49:3; 119:11; Proverbs 4:23-24; 10:20; 12:18; 15:2; 18:21; 21:23; 23:7; 25:21; 31:26; Matthew 12:33-37; Luke 6:45; Ephesians 4:14; Colossians 3:16; James 1:27-28; 3:6-10.)

I Call You When I Need You Weed

You don't hear from The I Call You When I Need You Weed for a long time, and then it suddenly appears full-grown when it wants something I have. The I Call You When I Need You Weed takes from the friendship what it wants and then ignores the friend until another need arises. As with the I-Me Weed, selfishness is the source of the I Call You When I Need You Weed. Removal of this weed includes choosing to love my friend as myself (Mark 12:28-33), being more concerned about her needs than mine (Philippians 2:3-4), praying for a heart that desires to honor others. (See Leviticus 19:18; Matthew 5:43; Mark 12:33; Romans 2:6-8; 12:10; 13:7; Philippians 2:3-4; Hebrews 13:1; 2 Peter 1:7-11.)

Mom says. regardless of weeds' exterior appearances. all come from the same source or taproot: pride. the first of the six things the Lord hates (Proverbs 6:1). Pride creates disharmony in the friendship garden. while humility. the opposite of pride. generates an atmosphere of peace and harmony. The most effective time to remove weeds in my friendship garden is when they are young. tender. and actively growing—and I can only do this in the Lord's strength. As James 4:6. the spiritual weed killer. is applied to the invading weeds. my friendship garden can produce fabulous bouquets.

As we wrapped up our conversation. Mom reminded me Jesus pleads in John 17:20-21. "I do not ask for these only, but also for those who will believe in me through their word, that they may all be one, just as you, Father, are in me, and I in you, that they also may be in us, so that the world may believe you have sent me." She challenged me to be quick to remove weeds from my friendship garden so the watching world will observe the love of God in my friendships (John 13:35).

168 Topic: No Favorites

Tonight was our weekly 168 meeting. Pastor John chose the topic of impartiality to challenge us to be willing to follow the biblical model of "loving our neighbor as ourselves" (James 2:8). He shared that, according to Webster's Dictionary, impartiality means "not partial or biased." To understand impartiality you must first see Webster's definition of partial—the action of being "biased or prejudiced in favor of one person, group, side over another." Practically speaking, Christians are not to have favorites.

Impartiality

James 2:1-17 challenges Christians to reject the sin of partiality (2:9) by focusing on how the Lord Jesus, the King of the universe, chose to arrive on earth.
- He was born in a stable (Luke 2:7).
- His earthly father was a simple carpenter (Matthew 1:1-16).
- He lived in the humble village of Nazareth for 30 years (Matthew 2:19-23; Luke 2:39).
- He chose men working in a variety of careers, including fishermen, as His disciples (Matthew 18:22; Mark 1:16-20).
- He ministered in Galilee and Samaria, two communities notoriously looked down on by Israel's leaders (Matthew 1:23-25; John 4).
- He ate with tax collectors and sinners (Matthew 9:10-12).
- He associated with women of questionable reputation (John 4:1-26; 8:1-11).

Contrast Between the Rich and the Poor

Pastor John compared the church's reaction to the rich and the poor (James 2:2-4). He stated the church is to be a classless society since its primary concern is to fulfill the royal law and "love your neighbor as yourself" (2:8). He said that he did some research using The MacArthur Study Bible and its note says, "James is not promoting some kind of emotional affection for oneself. Self-love is clearly a sin (2 Timothy 3:2). Instead, the command is to try to meet the physical and spiritual needs of one's neighbors. Our neighbors are all who are within the sphere of our influence (Luke 10:30-37). We're to use the same intensity and concern as we naturally have for ourselves (Philippians 2:3-4)." So what? As he concluded our Bible study, he challenged us to concentrate on fulfilling the royal law by loving our neighbor as ourselves. I was convicted! I am so consumed with trying to fix my relationship with Bekka that I had not considered my hF may want me to direct my time and energy to the "neighbors" whom I could demonstrate impartiality to—the shy girl in my family group in Nutrition class, some of the teens from low income families in our youth group, the aging in our church, and the homeless people who come to our church's soup kitchen. My heart was tender as Pastor John allowed us time for personal prayer . . .

Dear hF, thank you for this study on impartiality. Please forgive me for being so consumed about my relationship with Bekka that I've failed to admit that maybe You want me to spend more time with others. I love her and want to reconcile with her. I also love You and want to fulfill your Royal Law. Please give me Your wisdom to know how to be impartial and to include those in my friendship garden those others may reject. In Your name I pray, amen.

Bethany and I are working on developing a heart of contentment as a part of our small group time. <u>Contentment</u> means.
"satisfied with what one is or has; not wanting anything else,"
according to Webster's. Tonight I learned Scripture teaches
that godliness with contentment is great gain (Psalm 37:16;
1 Timothy 6:6).
Knowing God's promises should lead to contentment (Hebrews 13:5).
Those who seek contentment from money are never satisfied
(Ecclesiastes 5:10). Believers are instructed to show contentment
in the job God calls them to (1 Corinthians 7:20), with their
wages (Luke 3:14), with their possessions (Hebrews 13:5), and
with the food and clothing they have (1 Timothy 6:8).
Bethany took the book <u>Becoming a Woman Who Pleases God</u>
and made it relate to teen girls. She put together a plan for
young women who want to be godly. This involves:
• getting rid of unneeded cares (1 Peter 5: 7-10).
• checking my gratitude (Colossians 3:12-17).
• releasing my anxieties and trusting in my hF (Psalm 55:22).
• obeying God's Word (Jeremiah 15:16).
Also. it means:
• joyfully submitting to my heavenly Father (Colossians 3:18).
• willingly submitting to those in authority (Ephesians 5:21. 6:1-2;
   James 4:7; 1. Peter 3:13);
• practicing self-control. kindness. along with having a pure
   heart and mind (Titus 2:5).
(If I didn't know better I would think Bethany looked in my
scrapbook because she then shared that two qualities—flexibility
and forgiveness—will affect my ability to be satisfied in life.)

Dear Lord, please help me to apply Philippians 4:11 and Hebrews 13:5 to my life and relationship with Bekka. I don't want to disobey you; I want to be forgiving as YW says. And please forgive me for my sins. I want to be content in all circumstances—even those I don't understand. You know I can't keep a contented heart, be flexible, or extend forgiveness in my own strength. I'm thankful I can do all things through You (Philippians 4:13). In Your name I pray, amen.

? 4 U

Many Scriptures give descriptions of the behaviors a friend should practice.

Check out these and jot down your thoughts:

Ephesians 5:21, Colossians 3:13, and 1 Thessalonians 5:11, 14 (what qualities should I show as a friend?)

Proverbs 17:17 and 18:24

John 4

Have I chosen my friends wisely? Am I treating any friendship as if it were an idol?

Journal about how you're applying the Scriptures about being—or having—a BFF.

Any other Scriptures you've found? Write them here:

MSG BOD

We began a new topic in Health today. smart eating. Mrs. T introduced it by asking. "Do you eat to live or live to eat?" After a lively discussion. we figure most of us do both. The facts fall into three groups. We eat because: we need energy. otherwise. we couldn't concentrate to study or have stamina to work or play.

Our bodies are used to eating. Conditioning shapes people's behavior. Some examples of food conditioning are eating about the same time each day. wanting certain foods at a particular activity (like popcorn at a movie. and expecting certain food when we visit relatives or friends).
Food's often at the center of a celebration (birthday or holidays). Many happy memories we have about an event are associated with the food served.

Smart Eating Lecture. Mrs. T. Family Living. Notes
Nutrients. Smart eating is based on our ability to under-stand these. Nutrients are substances that nourish or support the body. Nutrient density is the ratio of nutrients in a food to number of calories. The more nutrients in relation to calories. the higher the nutrient density. If you eat a lot of foods with low nutrient density. you may feel full without getting the nutrients your body needs.

(Check my Nutrient Density from today's meals.)
Since nutrients are grouped into six categories. pro-teins. carbohydrates. fats. vitamins. minerals. and water. we'll divided the class into six groups and assign a nutrient to each. Using the course text and the Internet to locate facts about each. we'll share find-ings in class tomorrow. See attached discussion guide.

A GUIDE TO SMART EATING

Nutrient: Protein
Definition: Found in every cell of the body, protein helps grow and repair tissue. Between 3 and 5 percent of body protein needs to be replaced daily. All protein is made up of amino acids. There are about 20 amino acids. Eight are known as essential amino acids. These are amino acids that the body can't make itself and must get from the daily diet.
Source: Most food from animal sources contains all 8 essential amino acids; these are said to contain complete protein. Meat, fish, poultry, eggs, milk, cheese, and yogurt are sources of complete protein. Many vegetable foods contain only some of the essential amino acids. Such food supplies incomplete protein. Peanut butter, nuts, seeds, and dried beans contain most of the essential amino acids and are good sources of incomplete protein.

I need to reduce my
sugar and increase my fiber.

Nutrient: Carbohydrates
Definition: The main source of the body's energy is carbohydrates. The body changes carbs into glucose used as fuel in cells.
Source: There are three kinds of carbohydrates: sugar, starch, and fiber. Sugar is the simplest carbohydrate and breaks down quickly in the body. Starch is more complex and takes longer to break down. Fiber is a complex carbohydrate. It's sometimes called roughage. Though it does not supply energy and can't be broken down by the body, it's very necessary because it helps move food and waste through the digestive system.
Sugar found in fruit is called fructose. Beets, sweet potatoes, and peas are also sources of sugar. Milk contains a natural sugar called lactose. Refined or processed sugar is used in the manufacture of soda, candy, and pastry (pies, cakes, and cookies). Corn syrup, sucrose, dextrose, and honey are all forms of sugar. It's added to many foods.
Rice, bread, pasta products, and vegetables such as potatoes and corn are good sources of starch.
Whole-grain breads and cereals, vegetables and fruits, especially their seeds and peels, are sources of fiber.

Nutrient: Fats

Definition: Fat provides more than twice as much energy as carbohydrates. Fat also carries fat-soluble vitamins throughout the body. Fats can be saturated, trans, monounsaturated or polyunsaturated.

Saturated fats are solid at room temperature. They occur naturally in many foods. The majority come from animal sources, including meat and dairy products. Examples are fatty beef, lamb, pork, poultry with skin, beef fat (tallow), lard, cream, butter, cheese, and other dairy products made from whole or reduced-fat (2 percent) milk. These foods also contain dietary cholesterol. The American Heart Association recommends limiting the amount of saturated fats you eat to less than 7 percent of total daily calories. That means, for example, if you need about 2,000 calories a day, no more than 140 of them should come from saturated fats. That's about 16 grams of saturated fats a day.

Trans fats (or trans fatty acids) are created in an industrial process that adds hydrogen to liquid vegetable oils to make them more solid. Another name for trans

Calculate intake of SatFat!

fats is "partially hydrogenated oils." Look for them on the ingredient list on food packages. Trans fats raise your "bad" (LDL) cholesterol levels and lower your "good" (HDL) cholesterol levels. Eating trans fats increases your risk of developing heart disease and stroke. It's also associated with a higher risk of developing type 2 diabetes. Trans fats can be found in many foods—but especially in fried foods like French fries and doughnuts, and baked goods including pastries, pie crusts, biscuits, pizza dough, cookies, crackers, and stick margarines and shortenings. You can determine the amount of trans fats in a particular packaged food by looking at the Nutrition Facts label. You can also spot trans fats by reading ingredient lists and looking for the ingredients referred to as "partially hydrogenated oils."

Monounsaturated (MUFAs) and polyunsaturated fats (PUFAs) or oils are liquid at room temperature but start to turn solid when chilled. Olive oil is an example of a kind of oil that contains monounsaturated fats. PUFAs contain some fatty acids that are necessary for health. They are called essential fatty acids.

The MUFAs and PUFAs found in fish, nuts, and vegetable oils don't raise the "bad" cholesterol levels in the blood. From a chemical standpoint, monounsaturated fats have one double-bonded (unsaturated) carbon in the molecule. While polyunsaturated fats are simply fats that have more than one double-bonded (unsaturated) carbon in the molecule. Most of the fats you eat should be mono or polyunsaturated. Monounsaturated fats can have a beneficial effect on your health when eaten in moderation and when used to replace saturated fats or trans fats.

Monounsaturated fats can help reduce bad cholesterol levels in your blood and lower your risk of heart disease and stroke. They also provide nutrients to help develop and maintain your body's cells. Monounsaturated fats are also typically high in vitamin E, an antioxidant vitamin.

Polyunsaturated fats can have a beneficial effect on your health when consumed in moderation and when used to replace saturated fats or trans fats. Polyunsaturated fats can help reduce the cholesterol levels in your blood and lower your risk of heart disease. They also provide essential fats that your body needs but can't produce itself—such as omega-6 and omega-3. Your body needs these fats for healthy cell development. Omega-6 and omega-3 play a crucial role in brain function and in the normal growth and development of your body. According to www.americanheart.org: Foods high in polyunsaturated fat include a number of vegetable oils, including soybean oil, corn oil and safflower oil, as well as fatty fish such as salmon, mackerel, herring and trout. Other sources include some nuts and seeds."

Cholesterol is a fat-like substance that is made in the liver and is found in saturated fats. When the body has too much cholesterol, it's deposited along the artery walls. When the arteries become clogged, the blood can't flow easily. This can cause heart attacks and strokes.

Polyunsaturated fats can have a beneficial effect on your health when ~~consumed in moderation and when used to replace saturated fats or trans~~ fats. Polyunsaturated fats can help reduce the cholesterol levels in your blood and lower your risk of heart disease. They also provide essential ~~fats that your body needs but can't produce itself—such as omega-6 and~~ omega-3. Your body needs these fats for healthy cell development. Omega-6 and omega-3 play a crucial role in brain function and in the normal ~~growth and development of your body.~~ According to www.americanheart. org: Foods high in polyunsaturated fat include a number of vegetable oils. including soybean oil. corn oil and safflower oil. as well as fatty fish such as salmon. mackerel. herring and trout. ~~Other sources include some nuts and seeds.~~

Cholesterol is a fat-like substance that is made in the liver and is found in saturated fats. ~~When the body has too much cholesterol. it's deposited~~ along the artery walls. When the arteries become clogged. the blood can't flow easily. This can cause heart attacks and strokes.

The MUFAs and PUFAs found in fish. nuts. and vegetable oils don't raise the "bad" cholesterol levels in the blood. From a chemical standpoint. monoun- saturated fats have one double-bonded (unsaturated) carbon in the mol- ~~ecule. while polyunsaturated fats are simply fats that have more than one~~ double-bonded (unsaturated) carbon in the molecule. Most of the fats you eat should be mono or polyunsaturated. ~~Monounsaturated fats can have a beneficial effect on your health when eaten in moderation and when used~~ to replace saturated fats or trans fats.

Monounsaturated fats can help reduce bad cholesterol levels in your blood ~~and lower your risk of heart disease and stroke.~~ They also provide nutri- ents to help develop and maintain your body's cells. Monounsaturated fats are also typically high in vitamin E. an antioxidant vitamin. Source: Fats occur naturally in many foods. ~~The majority come from animal~~ sources such as meat and dairy products. Many bakery items (donuts. cook- ies. cakes. etc.) and fried foods contain high levels of fats.

Nutrient: Vitamins
Definition: The nutrients called vitamins are necessary for the mainte-
nance, growth, and repair of the body. They are divided into fat-soluble
and water-soluble vitamins.
Vitamins A, D, E, and K are fat-soluble; they dissolve in fat. Because the
body can store what it does not immediately need, it's possible to overdose
on vitamins A and D if you take large doses of vitamin supplements.
Vitamins B and C are water-soluble; they dissolve in your body fluids. Since
the body does not store water-soluble vitamins any unneeded ones are elimi-
nated with body waste.
Since vitamins work with other nutrients in the body, the lack of a specific
vitamin in the diet may affect the effectiveness of another nutrient.
Source: Though there are many vitamin pills and supplements available it's
best to get vitamins from consuming foods. Vitamin pills and supplements can
give you too much of one vitamin. This can create in an imbalance in the
body. I created a chart to define and describe the sources of the common
vitamins so that I can easily refer to it.

Vitamin	Definition	Source
B The B Vitamins are a group of related vitamins often called the B-complex vita-mins. They are Thiamin, Ribofla-vin, and Niacin.	Helps release the energy in nutrients. Keeps the appetite and digestion normal. Aids in keeping the nervous system healthy. Assists in promoting smooth skin.	Milk. Milk products. Whole grain and enriched grain products. Meats. Vegetables.
C Sometimes called ascorbic acid.	Helps maintain teeth, bones, and certain blood vessels. Is destroyed by heat, exposure to the air, and large amounts of water.	Citrus fruits. Potatoes. Tomatoes. Cabbage. Strawberries.

A	Helps maintain healthy skin. Aids in helping the eyes adjust to darkness.	Deep-yellow and dark-green leafy vegetables. Fruits.
D Sometimes called the sunshine vitamin.	The body makes Vitamin D when the skin is exposed to sunlight. Helps the body use calcium and phosphorus to build strong bones and teeth.	Is added to most milk.
E	Helps protect cell tissues from being damaged by too much oxygen.	Found in whole grains.
K	Aids in the clotting of blood.	Manufactured by the body.

Nutrient:	Minerals
Definition:	The body needs only a small amount of minerals. Minerals help the nutrients and body processes to function. Since the vitamin chart is such a handy reference tool. I decided to also create one for minerals.

Nutrient:	Minerals	
		Source
Calcium	Important for strong bones and teeth. Almost 99 percent of the calcium in the body is stored in the bones and the teeth. Calcium helps the blood to clot. the muscles to contract. and the nerves to send messages. Calcium may also help blood pressure.	Milk and dairy food. Seafood. Green leafy vegetables.

Phosphorus	The body needs more calcium than phosphorus. Phosphorus deficiency is rare because this mineral is found in most foods, especially carbonated beverages. Excessive amounts of phosphorus interfere with calcium intake. A diet consisting of junk food is a common culprit. Vitamin D increases the effectiveness of phosphorus.	Found in most foods, especially carbonated beverages.
Iron	Found in red blood cells. Carries oxygen through the body. Turns food into energy. Anemia is a condition caused by a lack of iron in the blood.	Meat. Eggs. Green-leafy vegetables. Whole grains. Enriched cereals.
Iodine	Helps the thyroid gland make the hormone that promotes mental and physical growth. Needed only in trace amounts.	Iodized salt. Seafood. Asparagus, garlic, mushrooms, and spinach.
Sodium (salt)	Assists in controlling the body's water balance. Needed for stomach, nerve, and muscle function. Table salt is known as sodium chloride. Too much sodium chloride may contribute to high blood pressure or hypertension.	Almost all foods contain some sodium.

| Potassium | Important for a healthy nervous system and a regular heart rhythm. Helps prevent strokes. Aids in proper muscle contraction. Works with sodium to control the body's water balance. | Dairy foods. Fish. Fruit. Beans (legumes). Vegetables. Whole grains. |
| Trace Elements | Other minerals needed by the body in very small quantities. | Examples are copper and zinc. |

Source: As with vitamins, there are many mineral supplements available. Again, it's best to get minerals from consuming foods.

Drink more water, less soda—yikes!

| Nutrient: | Water |
| Definition: | The human body is two-thirds water. Water is an essential nutrient that affects every function of the body. It helps transport nutrients and waste products in and out of the cells. It's necessary for all digestive, absorption, circulatory, and excretory functions. It also is necessary for the absorption of water-soluble vitamins. Water helps maintain the correct body temperature. Death occurs within 3 to 4 days if the body does not have water. |

Source: By drinking at least eight 8-ounce glasses of water a day you can ensure that your body has all it needs to maintain good health. You lose water in perspiration, urine, and by breathing. Drinking water throughout the day helps to replace what is lost.

Healthy Diet. Lecture Notes.
Mrs. Titus

Nutritional requirements

Our bodies have specific nutritional requirements in order to function properly.

What to eat

A variety of foods are necessary to nourish us—meats. eggs. grain foods (breads. cereals. pastas). fruits. vegetables. and dairy products. as well as fats. oils. and sugars in moderate amounts. No one food is more or less important than the others; they are all needed and they all help one another nourish us.

Meats and eggs supply the protein necessary to build strong bodies and maintain body tissue. They. as well as the essential B vitamins. are also an abundant source of iron needed for rich red blood and the prevention of anemia. The word protein comes from the Greek for "first" and should be the first criteria when planning meals. The grain foods supply vigor and energy because of the carbohydrates. sugars. and starches they contain as well as significant amounts of the B vitamins. thiamine. niacin. and riboflavin.

A healthy diet balances the number of calories you eat with the number of calories you burn. It emphasizes eating vegetables. fruits. whole-grain/high-fiber foods. fat-free and low-fat dairy products. lean meats. poultry. fish (at least twice a week) and limiting your saturated fat. trans fat. and cholesterol. Also. drink fewer beverages and eat fewer foods with added sugars; choose and prepare foods with little or no salt.

Avoid

Work in groups to complete a chart of foods that promote smart eating.

This is a copy of our group's findings:

Body-Smart Eating

Too much sugar	Read ingredient labels.
	Buy fresh fruits or frozen fruits.
	Reduce the amount of sugar you use when you prepare food at home by adjusting the recipes you now use and trying new ones.
	Prepare foods at home instead of eating commercially prepared ones that are usually higher in sugar.
	Eat fresh fruit instead of something sweet for snacks and desserts.
Too much fat	Steam, boil, or bake vegetables.
	Season vegetables with herbs and spices in place of butter or margarine.
	Choose lean cuts of meats.
	Roast, bake, broil, or grill meat, poultry, or fish.
	Substitute plain low-fat yogurt, cottage cheese, or buttermilk in recipes calling for sour cream or mayonnaise.
Too much salt	Limit the amount of fast foods and snacks you eat.
	Look for recipes with reduced salt.
	Try adding new spices and herbs instead of salt when cooking.
	Taste your food before you salt it.
	Limit the amount of condiments (like ketchup) that you use.
Too many sodas	Drink milk instead of carbonated beverages.
	Remember that not only do sodas lack calcium; they also contain large quantities of phosphorus. Too much phosphorus can make it difficult for the body to absorb the calcium that the teenage body needs.

How Much to Eat?

Day 2--How Much to Eat

"When you stand on the scale and observe the weight that it records, what is your response?" "Would you consider yourself fit or fat?" The media tells us "Thin is in!"

Some teens, though slim, are dissatisfied with their weight and consider themselves fat.

A teen with anorexia nervosa has the constant fear of becoming extremely overweight or fat and will not eat or will eat very little.

Continuing preoccupation with one's weight can lead to two potentially dangerous eating disorders—anorexia nervosa and bulimia.

Bulimia is another serious eating disorder.

The photos accompanying the definitions of the eating disorders were crazy scary!

Before this next slide, Mrs T reminded us that help is available, and if one of our friends shows symptoms of eating disorders we should encourage them to see the school nurse, their counselor, or a health professional.

Persons suffering bulimia eat large amounts of food (binges) and then force vomit, believing purging will help them stay slim.

A healthy weight is the weight your body naturally settles into when you consistently eat a nutritious diet, are physically active, and balance the calories you eat with the physical activity.

Standard height and weight charts published by reputable organizations are helpful. Reaching a specific weight is not as important as the lifestyle changes you make to become healthy.

Calories

Food energy is measured in calories. The number of calories teens need depends on their age, gender, size, weight, and the amount of activity in their lives.

An active teen = physical activity equal to walking more than 3 miles per day at 3 to 4 miles per hour in addition to the physical activity associated with typical day-to-day life.

An active teen girl (14-18) needs about 2400 calories per day.

Teens whose lifestyle includes only the light physical activity associated with typical day-to-day life are categorized as being sedentary.

These teens should consume about 1800 calories per day.

Calorie charts display how many calories certain foods contain. When using a calorie chart we need to know the serving size and how the food was prepared.

French fries contain more calories than a baked potato.

Keeping a record of calorie intake for a week will give a good idea of how smart your eating patterns are.

Body mass index (BMI) determines obesity. To calculate, get an accurate weight and height measurement.

Partner work: calculate BMI

As my partner and I completed our BMI and compared them to the charts distributed by the National Center for Health Statistics that Mrs. T provided. I was reminded that though the charts are helpful tools, it's GW that reminds me that my body needs to be healthy to serve Him to my max! My study in Proverbs 31:10-31 challenged me to be energetic (31:13-16, 19-20, 14, 17) and physically fit (31:17). Romans 12:1-2 reminds me that I'm to yield my body so that it's an instrument of righteousness is to be yielded to God and that media should not set my standards. 1 Corinthians 3:16-17 and 6:19-20 clearly describe my body as God's, where His Holy Spirit dwells. I must be careful that I don't develop any eating habits that will damage God's body.

BMI CHART FOR: _____

Instruction   My Measurements

1. Weigh yourself
2. Write down your weight in pounds.
3. Measure yourself in inches
4. Divide your weight by your
    height in inches.
5. Divide the answer from step 4 by
    your height in inches.
6. Multiply the answer from step 5 by 703.
    The resulting number is your BMI.
7. Compare the results with a reliable growth
    chart such as the ones available from the
    National Center for Health Statistics
    (www.cdc.gov/growthcharts).

HF, thanks for what I learned about "smart eating." Mom plans nutritious menus and makes meal times special. Thank You for giving me a mom who's helping me learn those skills. I know my BMI is in the "healthy range" because she helps me select healthy foods I like. Your Word says you paid the high price for our bodies. I want to always use my body to honor You. Thank You, Lord Jesus, amen.

As our group gathered together. Bethany prayed and asked about our week.
Bethany's taking Nutrition at The Master's College. We compared what we're learning. I described some classmates' reactions to BMI project. She LOL and shared our topic for night: Spiritual Nutritional Requirements.

Just as a dietary plan is necessary for sound nutrition. so an intentional spiritual dietary plan is as essential to our spiritual nutrition.

(I love the way she transitions into the spiritual focus our small group times should have)

Find 1 Peter 2:2-3. Read together. According to NT prof Jackson. "spiritual growth is marked by a craving for and a delight in God's Word. with the intensity with which a baby craves milk. Fill in the blanks to answer smart spiritual nutrition practices:

A Christian develops a desire for the truth of God's Word by:
remembering his life's source ("The word of the LORD endures forever"—1 Peter 1:25).
eliminating sin from his life ("Laying aside all malice and all guile and hypocrisy, and envy and all slander"—1 Peter 2:1).
admitting his need for God's truth ("... as newborn babes"—1 Peter 2:2).
pursuing spiritual growth ("...that you may grow thereby"—1 Peter 2:2).
surveying his blessings ("Lord is gracious"—1 Peter 2:3)."

The relationship between physical and spiritual nutrition: When we make sound nutritional choices, we have the opportunity to dramatically reduce our risk for many health challenges. The same is true in our spiritual life. When we practice smart spiritual nutrition by choosing to read and practice God's Word, spiritual vitality results. Psalm 119 is an excellent Spiritual Nutrition Guide. List all of the things that God's Word can do in our lives. God's Word is a...

source of blessing (vv. 1-8).
challenge to holiness (vv. 9-16).
teacher (vv. 17-24).
source of strength and renewal (vv. 25-32).
direction for life priorities (vv. 33-40).
reminder of God's unfailing love (vv. 41-48).
comfort in suffering (vv. 49-56).
portion (vv. 57-64).
standard for correction (vv. 65-72).
source of consolation (vv. 73-80).

We ran out of time before we ran out of verses so we committed to complete the list by studying all 176 verses. We'll share our findings with one another the next time we're together.

Thank You that Your Word teaches me that, while it's important that I take good care of the body You gave me, it's also important for me to nourish my spiritual vitality. I pray You'll help me improve both my physical and spiritual nutritional habits.

?4U

To dos for teen girls include:

How does the principle of physically fit apply to life? List practical ways to apply; pray for God's help in applying.

Conduct an Internet search to locate current government plans for smart eating.

Develop a weekly plan that helps me practice smart eating.

Evaluate food choices at the end of the week; smart eater this week?

What changes, if any, to improve eating plan next week?

Use resources on www.americanheart.org to calculate daily fat limits.

Learn how to read and understand food labels for smarter food choices. Study several labels of foods eaten regularly and complete the chart below for each food.

Analyzing Food Labels — A Tool to Eating Smarter

Record the size of a single serving (1 tablespoon. 1/4 cup, etc.).	A single serving of this food (insert measurement) =
Record the number of calories per serving.	The number of calories per serving =
Record the number of servings you actually eat in a day.	The number of servings I eat in a day =
Multiply the number of calories per serving by the number of servings you actually eat in a day.	The number of calories per serving multiplied by the number of servings I actually consume in a day =
Record the number of grams of fat for one serving of this food.	The number of grams of fat for one serving of this food =

Multiply the number of grams of fat per serving by the number of servings you actually eat in a day.	The number of grams of fat per serving multiplied by the number of servings I actually consume in a day =
Divide the total number of calories from this food eaten daily by 2000. Move the decimal point to the right to create a %.	The total number of calories I eat from this food in a day by 2000 = %.
Daily fat intake should be between 56-76 grams per day. Saturated fat should comprise 16 grams or less of the daily total fat intake. Compare the total number of grams of fat per serving with the number you eat from this food.	The total number of grams of fat per serving I intake from this food =
The total number of grams of saturated fat per serving I intake from this food	
How much cholesterol does this food contain?	The amount of cholesterol contained in this food =
The % Daily Value (DV) section of the label tells you the percent of nutrient in a single serving. What % of your DV comes from a serving of this food?	The % of my DV that comes from a serving of this food =
Evaluate the quality of this food choice.	If I choose to eat this food am I making a smart food choice? Why or why not?

Research anorexia nervosa and bulimia. Describe the characteristics of each.

Support a healthy response to "Thin is in!"? with facts:

Strategies that help a person with eating disorders learn to maintain a healthy body weight by eating smart are:
Complete the Body Mass Index (BMI) in this chapter.
Evaluate Body Mass Index (BMI).
Use the information to help me establish best body weight.
Be active; not sedentary.
Based on my response. I should eat _____ calories daily.
The number of calories I eat each week is _____. My evaluation of the number at the end of the week is:_____
My smart eating plan to keep my calories within the recommended calorie range is: _____

Take notes on the life of young Rebekah in Genesis 24:1-28. 58-67. Then:

List the tasks she performed that proved she was physically fit.

Write briefly how the tasks she completed affected her future and in what specific ways:

I followed Bethany's SG format and created my own Spiritual Nutrition Guide. I carefully analyzed Psalm 119 and listed all the roles God's Word can fulfill in my life. I think every teen girl should do this and post it on a sheet of paper in her home. where she can see it.

L8$

Happened this week: It's always a blessing to have an assignment in one class that dovetails with an assignment in another. We started a new topic in our sociology class that connects with assignments in my econ class. It has a catchy title. "Too Much Month at the End of the Money?" and is focused on learning how to manage our financial resources.

We all laughed when the teacher mentioned our financial resources since most of us didn't consider we have any. However. as she continued her introduction. we learned that we do have resources that we need to manage. As teens. we are all family members. Right now most of us depend on our parents for food. clothing. and most expenses.

One day we will be responsible for our own expenses. It's important to record what out parents have taught us about life and finances so that when we assume full responsibility for our expenses. we will not have too much month at the end of the money! The handout my soc teacher provided helped us to follow her PowerPoint. And then. the teacher gave us our first in-class assignment. We spent the remainder of our class period sharing what we had written. As other classmates shared their assignments. I realized how blessed I am to have been taught about finances at an early age. Many of my peers didn't have anything significant to share.

(Handout #1: Family Income) What My Parents Taught About $$
Sarah Joy Abramson

As soon as I could count. my parents introduced me to money. For example. they would give me the money to pay for an ice-cream cone in an amount that I would understand and then help me count the change when it was returned to me. They taught me to be account-able to them for the money that they had entrusted to me.

They talked with me about their values about money. Since they have been Christians for many years their values are based on the Bible. Some verses that they often talk about are

<u>Proverbs 13:11</u>—"Wealth gained hastily will dwindle. but whoever gathers little by little will increase it."

<u>Ecclesiastes 5:10</u>—"He who loves money will not be satisfied with money. nor he who loves wealth with his income: this also is vanity."

Matthew 6:24—"No one can serve two masters, for either he will hate the one and love the other, or he will be devoted to the one and despise the other. You cannot serve God and money."

Mark 12:40-42—"And he sat down opposite the treasury and watched the people putting money into the offering box. Many rich people put in large sums. And a poor widow came and put in two small copper coins, which make a penny. And he called his disciples to him and said to them, 'Truly, I say to you, this poor widow has put in more than all those who are contributing to the offering box. For they all contributed out of their abundance, but she out of her poverty has put in everything she had, all she had to live on.'"

1 Timothy 6:10—"For the love of money is a root of all kinds of evils. It's through this craving that some have wandered away from the faith and pierced themselves with many pangs."

Before I had a job, they gave me an allowance that was appropriate for my age. They also helped me learn how to manage the money. For example, I was to give at least 10 percent to the church, save at least 10 percent, and talk with them about my spending decisions. All my decisions were not good because I didn't always follow their advice. I am thankful that I could always talk to Dad and Mom about my spending decisions and how I either made a good or a poor choice. If I made a good choice I was complimented. If the choice was a poor one we talked about how I could improve the next time. And, they didn't rescue me with more money when the choice was poor. Instead, they helped me develop a solution to the consequences of my poor choice.

They helped me learn the differences between needs, wants, and wishes. This helped to prepare me to make good spending decisions when I began to earn my own money. As I completed this thought both time and space ran out.

HF, thank you that my parents have taught me about finances so I don't have to have too much month at the end of the money. Thank you for what your Word teaches me about money. Help me to always be a good manager of what you have given to me. In Your name I pray, amen.

Lecture Handout #2: Where $ Come From

Mrs. T began day 2 of our $$ study by asking the question. "Where does money come from?" Of course someone responded with "the ATM machine." When the laughter stopped Mrs. T referred us to the handout on our desks. We were to work together in partners and use our textbook and laptops to locate the sources of money.

Sources of $$

My partner and I found that the sources of money for most adults are:

Work. People usually earn most of their money by working. They earn wages or salaries in exchange for their labor.

Savings Accounts. When money is deposited in a savings account, the bank uses your money to earn more money. The bank pays you interest for the use of your money.

Stocks and Bonds. The purchase of *stocks and bonds* is a form of *investment*, the spending of money that can later bring in a larger sum of money. When a person buys stocks they actually own a small part of the business. The business pays its *shareholders a dividend*, which is a part of the company's profits. When a person buys bonds the person is actually lending money to the business or government agency that issued them. There is more risk involved in the purchase of *stocks and bonds* than in having a *savings account.* If the business or government agency does well, your investment increases. If it does not, you can actually lose a portion or all of your investment.

At the end of class Mrs. T collected our lecture handouts and said she would return them when they were graded. My partner and I were thankful we had used our time wisely ☺ ! I told Dad and Mom about our class project at dinner. They were pleased to learn of my interest in the sources of money and shared with me some of the investment decisions they have made. Since I have a new job our conversation eventually moved to the sources of my income.

Some Facts About My Income,
S. Abramson, period 1

My income comes from four sources: allowance, earnings from a job, interest from my savings account, and money gifts.

My allowance is the money my parents give me. A portion of it is based on tasks I complete at home and a portion is a gift from them. I am not paid for all of the tasks I am responsible for. They are a part of being a member of the Abramson family. However, if I don't complete the tasks I am paid for, my allowance is reduced.

My savings. I have had a savings account since I began receiving an allowance. My parents always paid me in cash in one dollar bills because it was easy to separate my tithe and savings from the total amount. They always required that I tithe at least 10 percent of my allowance and save at least a dollar. It's fun to take the money to the bank, watch the amount grow, and receive interest. I learned early that the money I deposited was known as the principal and the interest rate is the amount of money the bank pays me for using my money. Once the money is in the bank I don't like to withdraw it.

My job. Before my current position as an administrative assistant for my mom, I babysat and worked at several other part-time jobs to earn additional spending money.

How I Landed My Current Job

My mom's a busy lady! She not only makes our home a refuge for Dad and me, she teaches younger women how to practice the Titus 2 principles in their lives, works in New Hope's Women's Ministries, and is a published author. Due to her many responsibilities she has an administrative assistant that works for her 10 hours a week. When her former administrative assistant moved out of the area, she began interviewing for a replacement. I asked her about me filling the position. She said she would be happy to consider me but I would need to proceed through the normal application process that included submitting a résumé, proving I have a Social Security Card, providing references, and undergoing an interview. She insisted that I do the research to learn the basics of how to find a job. I created a handout for Econ class that summarizes my research along with the strategies I used in the application and interview process. It's under the Econ Tab and titled "How to Land a Good Job—How to Prepare a Résumé"

How to Prepare a *Résumé*

A résumé is a detailed outline of my job experience, education, and any special skills, activities, or interests relevant to the job I am applying for. A good résumé gives the employer a positive picture of me. It should be well organized, word processed, and printed on résumé paper (I learned that cream is a better choice than white.). Depending on the prospective employer, I can also save it in a portable document format (PDF) and burn it to a CD—or even a DVD if I want to record some video. An Internet search provided me with some valuable pointers. Since I saved my résumé on my computer, I am able to customize it for any job I apply for.

Contacting References.

Since employers usually ask for references I compiled a list of people who I have worked for, teachers, and people I have ministered with at New Hope Community Church. I selected those people who could provide the most helpful information for the position I was applying for. I didn't place their names on my résumé but included the statement, "References Available Upon Request." I contacted the potential references before giving the names to my potential employer to make sure they were willing to recommend me. When I was hired I sent them a note handwritten on nice stationery.

The Interview.

The research I conducted on interviews all indicated that the first impression a prospective employer has about me is lasting. These tips helped me:

- *Be prepared* by learning everything I can about the organization for which I want to work. Though I know some things about Mom's ministry, some research (other than asking her) helped me to have a fairly good idea about my potential job responsibilities.
- *Be on time.* The church receptionist scheduled a specific time for the interview. Since I needed to travel to Mom's office at the church, I allowed extra driving time. It was a good thing I did. Traffic was heavy on the day of the interview.

- *Dress neatly*. I chose clothing that would be the right thing to wear to work if I already had the job. I also checked to see that the outfit was clean and in good repair. I know that all of the church staff follows a dress code established by the elders. My job interview research stated that it's important to dress in such a way that shows my awareness of and my willingness to comply with the organization's dress code. The research also indicated that a prospective employer assumes that you look your best on the day of the interview.
- *Be courteous and friendly*. Though it was a little weird, I shook hands with the interviewer (my mom) at the beginning and end of the interview. I smiled when the receptionist introduced me to her and didn't sit down until I was asked to do so. I looked directly at the interviewer when she was speaking.
- *Be direct and honest*. I tried to answer all of the interviewer's questions fully. I also attempted to make my experience and background appear as favorable as possible.
- *Show my interest*. I asked questions about the job. I let her know that I was very interested in the position.
- *Follow up*. At the conclusion of the interview, the interviewer said she had several additional applicants she was considering and would let me know her decision by the end of the week. That evening I wrote her a brief, handwritten note, thanking her for the time she invested in interviewing me and restating my interest in the position. I was genuinely surprised when I received a phone call telling me of all the applicants interviewed my qualifications best met the job description!

Lecture Handout # 3: Managing Your $$

Building a Budget

A *budget*, or *spending plan*, is simply a road map for using the money you have to its maximum potential. Designing a personal *budget*, or *spending plan*, is not difficult. However, to build a successful *budget* I must know my personal goals and determine my expenses.

Setting Personal Goals. Every successful spending plan is based on clearly defined personal goals—the things I really want. They can be short-term, like saving for a new pair of shoes, or long-term, such as having enough money to attend college. Most goals require more money than what I have right now. That is why goals must be written down. Once they are in place, I am ready to build my budget.

Building My Budget. I need to list my income and expenses to develop my budget or spending plan. I must know the following information to be successful:

My Income—allowance, salary, gifts, and loans.

Fixed Expenses—tithing, car insurance, gas, etc.

Variable Expenses—school supplies, my portion of my clothing budget, entertainment, gifts, etc.

Savings—an established percentage of each paycheck. This needs to be determined before any money is spent from the first paycheck.

Creating a Weekly Spending Plan. Once my income and expenses are determined, I need to chart them weekly. This step allows me to develop a *spending plan* or *budget*. Once I have charted my expenses for a month, I need to evaluate it to determine whether or not it's helping me reach my personal goals. Revision is necessary if there is too much month at the end of the money.☺

The next topic in Econ was a perfect complement to my socio class and my new job: "Managing Your Money." The teacher introduced it by stating, "Failing to have a budget is like trying to navigate through an unfamiliar city without a road map. You most likely will get lost." Her statement reminded me of Proverbs 29:18, "Where there is no revelation, the people cast off restraint, (or the people are discouraged)" (NIV).

Dear hF, please help me to be a good manager of the income You have given to me. Help my personal goals to reflect biblical principles for using my income so that You are pleased with my choices. In Your name I pray, amen.

Lecture Handout #4: Credit—Friend or Foe?

Facts About Establishing
 and Maintaining Good Credit
Sarah Abramson
Econ, Mrs. T

Establishing Credit

I was amazed that so many credit offers are designed for high school and college students. My Internet search yielded 19 companies and suggested that I compare the offers and apply for the credit card of my choice by filling out a secure online application.

If you don't have credit (or much credit), the key is to start small. One credit card or a small loan can get the ball rolling. But, make sure your lender reports your on-time payments to one of the three credit bureaus, Equifax (equifax.com), Experian^{SM} (experian.com) or TransUnion® (transunion.com)—and preferably to all three. If your on-time payments don't get reported, you're accumulating debt but not building credit. Only credit accounts that report your borrowing and repayment activity will count toward your credit history.

Today the topic of Credit was introduced in our Econ class. The teacher began with the question. "What is credit?" The discussion eventually ended with the statement that credit is basically a promise to pay in the future for what can be bought or purchased today. We concluded that credit can be a friend or foe depending on how It's used. The remainder of class time was spent on the instructions for tonight's home- work. Each student is to find facts about how to establish and maintain good credit. Using the Internet. I located a num- ber of useful facts. including at credit card companies pages called "cardmember services."

Some tips to help establish a good credit history are:
- When you get a card, always pay off the balance in full when the statement arrives. Paying off your balance in full shows the card company that you're fiscally responsible. You're using credit as it was intended: as a short-term loan.
- Pay on time. One of the most important steps in building and maintaining a solid credit history is to pay all of your bills on time each month. By paying on time, you're showing the lender or creditor that you have enough cash flow to cover your expenses. If you pay late and the creditor reports your late payment to the credit bureaus, it damages your credit history and lowers your credit score.

- Keep your total charges well within your credit limit. If you want to boost your credit history and credit score, you'll want to keep your total monthly charges well within your credit limit. Why? In calculating your credit score, you will be penalized if your balance is above that limit because it signals to creditors that you may be having financial difficulties and, thus, are a riskier borrower.

- Regularly read your credit report. (Credit bureaus will provide you with one free copy per year if you contact them.) One way to build a positive credit history is to make sure you know what information is being reported. Errors and negative information can damage your credit history and your credit score, so you will want to regularly check your credit report to see what was recorded.

- By establishing and maintaining a good credit history you will be able to borrow that money when you want it, at the most favorable terms and conditions being offered.

I asked my dad. "Does Romans 13:8 mean that a Christian should not borrow money or use credit?"

Dad smiled and invited me to sit down while he reached for his John MacArthur Study Bible. He shared that Exodus 22:25, Psalm 37:21, Matthew 5:42, and Luke 6:34 are some of many verses that permit and control the borrowing of money. Paul's point in Romans 13:8 is that all our financial obligations must be paid when they are due. (Dad also reminded me from a note in the study notes not to forget the second portion of the verse—that I am to love not only other Christians, but also non-Christians.) Rather than avoiding the use of credit I am to practice self-control (Galatians 5:23), examine my motive for using credit to make sure it's not because I am coveting what someone else has (Exodus 20:17), and make sure my purchases don't reflect a lack of contentment (Philippians 4:11; Hebrews 13:5). As we concluded our chat he suggested that he and I study the credit cards available to teens and that I apply for one. Now that I have a regular salary maybe it's time for me to build my credit history.

Building a High Credit Score

A credit score is a three-digit number that represents your entire credit history. Credit scores are designed to predict how risky you will be as a borrower and what your chances are of making good on loans and other financial obligations. The scoring system analyzes how you manage each piece of credit (such as credit card accounts, mortgage or home equity loans, car loans, school loans and other debt) and then calculates your credit score based on how you've handled your debts over time.

Different companies use different formulas to come up with a credit score. While all the formulas look at roughly the same information (things like your outstanding debts, whether you pay on time, whether you carry a balance), one formula may give more weight to certain factors than others, so different companies could assign you different credit scores.

With a FICO score, the most widely used model, these are the components that go into the calculation of your credit score:

- Payment history: 35 percent
- Amounts owed: 30 percent
- Length of credit history: 15 percent
- New credit: 10 percent
- Types of credit used: 10 percent

When it comes to building a high credit score, the most important thing you can do is pay all your bills on time. If you can pay your bills in full and avoid carrying balances on your credit cards, your credit score is likely to increase.

Thank You, Father, that I had so many resources available to help me with my homework assignment. I am grateful for what I learned from Dad's insight on the biblical principles relating to borrowing money. Thanks, too, that Dad is willing to allow me to begin to build my own credit history before I attend college. Help me to make credit my friend rather than my foe. In Your name I pray, amen.

Econ Lecture Handout #5: Consumer Decisions

❏ Note homework assignment! According to the law consumers have many rights. As a part of Mrs. T's presentation, she conducted a brief Internet search by entering the words consumer rights into the search engine. Numerous sources were displayed. She assigned each student to research two for homework and bring back the results tomorrow.

Becoming a Cool Consumer

One of the most important strategies leading to sound consumer choices is comparison shopping. Comparison shopping involves evaluating a number of competing products. As a class we compiled a list describing what we should consider when making a major purchase. The list included:

- Quality of workmanship
- Ease of use
- Conditions of the warranty (the manufacturer's terms of repairing or replacing the item if it does not perform according to its advertised expectations)
- The features that are most important to the consumer
- Cost of the item
- The importance of purchasing a name- brand item
- The best place to purchase the item—many choices are available such as retail and discount stores, catalogs, the Internet, thrift stores, and garage sales.
- The reputation of the place you choose to purchase the item
- The season of the year—it can affect what is available to buy and how much you will need to pay for it

While all of the criteria on our list, according to Mrs. T, are important, she reminded us that the process of comparison shopping should yield a satisfying purchase. However, it's not a good choice if the consumer really does not need the item.

The consumer decisions made by teens is the final topic our class investigated in learning how to manage our financial resources. Though it doesn't seem possible. teens play an important role in the economic system. When we work. we are a producer. helping to fulfill the wants and needs of consumers. When we save our money in a bank or invest in stocks and bonds. we are an investor. When we spend money. we are a consumer. A consumer is anyone who buys goods and services.

I thought about her words as I left class. They reminded me of the principle of economical found in Proverbs 31:18. The WTIP "perceives that her merchandise is profitable."

Dear hF, thank You that Your Word provides clear instructions about consumer decisions. Help me to be a WTIP by following the principle of economical in all of my consumer decisions. In Your name I pray, amen.

Econ Lecture Handout #6:
Writing a Consumer Concern Letter

The Next Step

If a store is unable to resolve a purchase-return problem, write to the company that manufactured the product. Mrs. T gave us some ideas of how to write a letter or e-mail, since some companies have a contact feature on their Web page:

- *Address* the correspondence to the person in charge of complaints at the company headquarters. You can probably get the name of the correct person to write to by phoning the company (contact information is usually on the label) or checking their Web site.
- *Word process* the correspondence. Be sure it's free of spelling and grammatical errors. If using the "contact" feature on their Web site, word-process the message in your word processing program, check the grammar and spelling, then copy and paste it into the contact portion of the Web site.
- *Keep* the correspondence brief, but make sure it contains:
    What you bought.
    Where you bought it.
    When you bought it.
    How much you paid for it.
    What is wrong.
    To whom you have already complained.
    A copy of the original sales receipt. Don't send the original.
    Your name, address (with the ZIP code), and phone number.
- *The tone* of the correspondence should be businesslike and polite.
- *Keep* a copy of the correspondence.
- *Follow up* with a second inquiry if you don't receive a response in a reasonable amount of time.

As we concluded our study of Consumer Decisions, the teacher posed the question, "What do you do when you have a problem with something you bought?" The first response was to review the labels or instruction book to see you are using the product properly. If so, then return it to the store and ask for the person who handles complaints. It's necessary to take the sales slip, tags, and labels. If possible, the product should be returned in its original bag or box. Mrs. T agreed with the response and reminded us of the importance of being polite even though we are unhappy with the product.

- *You may contact* one of the federal agencies responsible for enforcing consumer laws if the situation is not resolved to your satisfaction. An Internet search will give you contact information for the Office of Consumer Affairs (a part of the US Department of Commerce), the Federal Trade Commission, and your local Better Business Bureau.

❏ Note homework assignment! The final assignment for the study on learning how to manage our financial resources was to write a practice consumer concern letter and locate the addresses of the Office of Consumer Affairs, the Federal Trade Commission, and my local Better Business Bureau.

Thank You, Father, for all I've learned about how to manage my financial resources. I want my spending to reflect what I've learned (James 1:22). Help me remember to follow the correct steps to resolve issues and be polite. In Your name I pray, amen.

?4U

Locate Bible verses referencing money and write a description about what they teach about money and how to use it. Scripture search on the word *money*, using both a bound and electronic concordance. Format a chart like this to record findings.

Scripture	What the Verse Says to Me
1 Corinthians 4:1–2	I am to be a good manager of all of the resources God has given to me.

Understand the sources of money—*principal, savings accounts, interest rate, stocks, bonds, dividend, and shareholders* by researching them and recording the answers, and include a bibliography of the references.

Use the *"Building My Budget"* form in the Econ tab to record weekly income and expenses.

Investigate the meaning of common credit terms—Annual Percentage Rate (APR), Balance Transfer, Billing Cycle, Cardmember Agreement, Cash Advance, Credit History, Credit Limit, Credit Report, Credit Score, Default, FICO score, Finance Charges, Fixed Interest Rate, Fraud Alert, Grace Period, Identity Theft, Interest, Interest Rate, Introductory Rate, Late Fee, Minimum Payment, PIN (Personal Identification Number), Prime Rate, Zero Balance.

Search *consumer rights* online (some resources available to the consumer are included in my notebook). Make a list of the Web sites that appear most useful.

Develop a list of *comparison shopping* strategies to consider when making a major purchase.

Practice writing a consumer concern letter following the guidelines under "Crafting a Consumer Concern Letter." An Internet search gives guidelines for a standard business letter.

Locate addresses of the Office of Consumer Affairs, the Federal Trade Commission, and local Better Business Bureau and keep for ready reference.

Write:

I can apply the principle of *economical* to my life in the following ways:

• Ask God for the motivation to put the items on the list into action.
• Study the life of the widow in Mark 12:41–44.
• Identify the task she performed that proved she was economical.
• Describe how the task she completed affected her future

I Serve U?

Servanthood

Pastor John asked us to hold up our envelopes to make sure everyone had one. He revealed the contents—two letters—and asked us to turn our backs so we could open them privately. Once open, we were to create the first word that came to mind. One letter was an "E" and the second could either be an

When we came in tonight, each person received a sealed envelope to put in our Bibles. Some held the envelope up to the light to figure out what it contained. Others felt the envelope. Some whispered that it must be a gift card for yogurt, instructions for a scavenger hunt, or something else. Then the worship team began praise time.

"M" or a "W." Within a few seconds, he took a poll—how many formed the word WE? Only a few hands were raised (at least we were honest). The majority of the teens in the room, me included, created the word ME. He had our attention for his topic for the evening—<u>servanthood</u>.

This is the last topic Pastor John will speak on until after the holidays, so he began by asking some questions about our year: Did you accomplish all that you wanted to spiritually? Did you seek to serve others (a focus on the WE) or did you choose to think of ME? If you served the Lord, did you do it with gladness like Psalm 100 describes? Do you have the heart of a servant? (Pastor John describes a servant as being excited about making someone else successful.)

The body language of our group suggested that Pastor John had selected the wrong topic for the last session before the holidays. Even with the ME/WE discussion we had just completed the faces around me reflected, Huh? Me? A Servant?

Rather than using the traditional Christmas verses usually reviewed at this season of the year, Pastor John began his message with Mark 10:45: "For even the Son of Man did not come to be served, but to serve, and to give his life as a ransom for many" (NIV).

Elaborating, Pastor John got straight to the point. Our heavenly Father wants the same response from us as He did from Jesus. Jesus left heaven to serve and to give. Those who are in a part of the eternal family are to conform to Jesus' role model.

Having gotten our attention, he then moved to what the main focus of the Christmas season often is—gift giving. Reminding us of the ME/WE discussion, he focused on Mary of Bethany, a woman who gave a costly gift to Jesus. Directing us to Mark 14:3-9, and John 12:1-9, he began to describe a woman who gave all she could for the Lord.

Jesus and His disciples were in Bethany. Shortly before Jesus' death, they were having dinner in the house of Simon the Leper. Mary (John 12:3), the sister of Martha and Lazarus, came and anointed Jesus' head with expensive perfume contained in an alabaster flask. Since the flask, a long-necked bottle made out of a special type of marble to keep it fresh, needed opening, it's assumed that it was full. John 12:3 reports that the perfume was pure spikenard, a costly perfume from India and that Mary used it to anoint Jesus' feet. The anointing of the feet was a symbol of service and humility—something that we don't do very well in our twenty-first-century culture. The Gospel of Mark also describes the anointing—first His head (Mark 14:3) then His body (Mark 14:8).

At that point, Pastor John opened a jar of his wife's best perfumed cream and rubbed a bit on his hand. Soon the fragrance filled the room. Letting the aroma permeate our olfactory senses, he asked us to image how the room probably smelled as Mary anointed Jesus.

The reaction of the disciples was Pastor John's next point. Rather than complimenting Mary on her selfless action, they felt that it was a waste.

The amount of money was equivalent to a year's salary for the average worker, and they felt it could have been used for a better purpose (12:4–5). Jesus reprimanded them for their response and told them to cease their foolish conver-sation (14:6).

Pastor John turned his teaching to us and asked us how many times we misjudge the *(Wow. I need to pray for forgiveness about Bekka and others too)* generous actions of others, whether it's the use of time, talent, or resources. Our downward looks provided a strong affirmative answer.

Bringing the description to a conclusion we were reminded that Jesus affirmed Mary's actions (14:6–9). She served the Lord while she could (14:8). The result of Mary's service was far reaching (14:9). Her action would lead to a perpetual testimony that she loved her Lord, served, and worshipped Him. Pastor John then had several thoughts for us:

Answer these questions in my Quiet Time Journal.
Will you leave our gathering tonight as a ME person or a WE person? How will Mary's example of doing what she could influence your choices as you think about next year's choices? Mary's servant actions probably left a lingering fragrance in the room. When you complete an act of service is there a lingering pleasant reminder? Or do people remember that you completed the task but had a negative, complaining spirit? Think about Ephesians 2:10 and James 1:22—remember Jesus likes active Christians! What are you doing with your time? Do you need to maximize it?

Our last session before the holidays will help us focus on maximizing our time as we consider developing a Christian worldview, analyz-ing the principle of salt and light, and answering the question, "Should I be involved in a ministry?"

168 Topic:
Developing a Christian Worldview

At 168, after prayer, worship, and announcements we settled into the final session of the year. Pastor John began
the evening with a reminder of our group name, 168, and
our theme. The name stands for how many hours there are
in the week. We chose this name to remind us to make
the most of each day. Our theme is, "Every moment, every
breath, every opportunity for the glory of God" (taken
from Ephesians 5:15-21). He then asked us to consider the
question—"In light of our name and theme, how broad is your
world?"

He challenged us to apply our name and theme by becoming
aware of current events so that we have an accurate knowledge of topics being discussed by well-informed people. It's unlikely,
according to Pastor John, that we will have an opportunity to
influence others for Christ if we don't know what is going on.
Therefore, we should intentionally stimulate our minds spiritually
and intellectually. This spiritual and intellectual stimulation should
lead to the development of a personal Christian Worldview.
Since Pastor John had a number of points he wanted us to
remember from his message he gave us a handout.

Developing a Christian Worldview

Christian Worldview... a definition according to John MacArthur's book, *Think Biblically!*:

The Christian worldview sees and understands God the Creator and His creation—i.e. man and the world—primarily through the lens of God's special revelation, the Holy Scriptures, and secondarily through God's natural revelation in creation as interpreted by human reason and reconciled by and with Scripture, for the purpose of believing and behaving in accord with God's will and thereby, glorify God with one's mind and life, both now and in eternity.

A *Christian Worldview* will be helpful as you pursue a college education or a career:

- in *scholarship*. A *Christian Worldview* serves as a bright light reflecting the glory of God in the midst of intellectual darkness.
- in *evangelism*, to answer the questions and objections of the unbeliever.
- in *discipleship*, to inform and mature you as a true believer

We discussed the definition and why it's important for teens to develop a Christian Worldview before we leave high school. Pastor John helped us to define four areas:

in Christ, with regard to the implications and ramifications on one's Christian faith. According to *MacArthur's Study Bible*, this worldview provides a framework for understanding the world and all of its reality from God's perspective and orders one's life according to God's will,

Pastor John challenged us as WTIPs to broaden our world by developing a personal Christian Worldview. This process begins by cultivating our minds and elevating our thoughts. He believes that as we choose to do so, the principle of salt and light will be evident in our lives.

Some interesting facts from saltinstitute.org:

- French fries are boring without it. From my nutrition study in Health, I offered that salt is a *nutrient*, a substance that nourishes or supports the body, and that in moderation it's necessary for life and health.
- Several others recently completed a science project on salt. Pastor John had asked them to share some of their most important findings. They used colorful PowerPoint slides to report some interesting facts:
- Salt is used in greater quantities and for more applications than any other mineral.
- It has more than 14,000 uses, and everyone uses salt directly and indirectly.

People in the United States use more than 16 tons of salt during their lifetime. That is 402 pounds a year for each living American.

Only a small percentage of the 402 pounds are actually eaten.
[Keep a record of the amount of salt I eat daily for a week to make sure the quantity is moderate.]

The rest is used for water conditioning (yeah, soft water), animal nutrition, winter roadway safety, the manufacture of paper, the standardization of dye batches in textiles, cloud seeding for rain, and as an artist's supply.

According to www.saltinstitute.org, "Salt is one of the most commonly used seasonings in antiquity (Job 6:6). Its preservative powers made it an absolute necessity of life and, not surprisingly, endowed it with religious significance."

Salt was used for Israelite worship to season incense (Exodus 30:35) and all offerings were to be seasoned with salt (Leviticus 2:13; Ezekiel 43:24).

Numbers 18:19 and 2 Chronicles 13:5 find salt symbolizing the making of a covenant. Jesus, in the Sermon on the Mount, calls the people who listen to Him "the salt of the earth" (Matthew 5:13). *The*

MacArthur Study Bible offers a useful description of the phrase "if the salt loses its flavor, how shall it be seasoned?" Salt is both a preservative and a flavor enhancer.

No doubt its use as a preservative was Jesus' primary concern. Pure salt can't lose its flavor or effectiveness, but the salt that is common in the Dead Sea area is contaminated with gypsum and other minerals and may have a flat taste or be ineffective as a preservative. Such mineral salts were useful for little more than keeping footpaths free of vegetation, the *MacArthur Study Bible* says.

The *New Bible Dictionary* states, "Light is the word used in connection with joy, blessing, and life in contrast to sorrow, adversity, and death. At an early time it came to signify God's presence and favor (Psalm 27:1; Isaiah 9:2; 2 Corinthians 4:6) in contrast to God's judgment (Amos 5:18)."

"The principle of *salt and light* comes from combining the preserving power of the salt with the joy and blessing derived from light," say the authors of *Becoming a Woman Who Pleases God*. A WTIP's presence should produce joy and blessing, and at the same time offer a savoring and preserving influence in any environment.

Choosing to become a *servant* allows us to practically apply the principle of *salt and light*.

(Lord, please help me to live up to the meaning of my middle name!)
Bringing this portion of our discussion to a close, Pastor John said that in our selfish society it's difficult for us to grasp why being a servant is good for us. The Christians' life is not about us pleasing ourselves but rather living in such a way that we glorify God. When we focus on allowing Him to be the Lord of our lives then we will become salt and light in a decaying, dark world. Choosing to do so will motivate us to be servants in the world as His representatives. This statement introduced his final point for the evening, ministry involvement.

As Pastor John began to speak of ministry involvement, he reminded us of Christ's example of coming to serve instead of being served. If we are only taking in the Word of God and coming to senior high group for the fun activities then we are consumers of the Word instead of doers of it. This is the opposite of what James 1:22 teaches. If we are going to be a "doer of the word" then we will be involved in a ministry.

At the same time, Pastor John cautioned, it's our responsibility to glorify God in our studies. Receiving a strong academic foundation will increase our ability to serve God more effectively in later years.

He then phrased the question many of us were thinking already—"how do you manage ministry, academics, and, for some of you, a job?" His answer was simple: we are to ask our heavenly Father to help us balance our lives. His PowerPoint slide helped:

"In your childhood,
did anyone ever jump off the
other end of the teeter-totter
without warning you?"

The first frame showed the illustration of a teeter-totter with a person sitting on each end. Pastor John asked. The downcast look of several suggested they had been guilty of causing the rude bump for the person on the other end by doing exactly what Pastor John described. He then suggested that both study and a personal ministry are necessary for a balanced Christian life. He encouraged us to place a job on the same side with study because both school and work is our means for gaining knowl-edge and experience to more effectively serve God in the future. From his personal experience. he said it's pos-sible to do both. The only time conflict between study and ministry arose for him was when he chose to waste his time or failed to discipline him-self in his studies that then created a crisis management situation.

A high priority on studies is found in Colossians 3:23–24; 2 Thessalonians 3:7–8. Paul worked hard at his vocation and carried on his ministry.

God calls us to study and to minister. Keeping that concept in mind gives us motivation, purpose, and a strong foundation for a lifestyle that pleases God.

Divide into our guy and girl groups to talk about how what we have learned applies specifically to our gender. Before moving, let's quiet ourselves and commit what we learned to the Lord.

Forgive me, Father, for practicing crisis management. Help me to use the good management skills I have learned from Dad, Mom, and Mrs. T.

HF, I like to have things done for me. I'm embarrassed I formed the word ME from the letters in the envelope. Help me have a greater desire to follow Your model as a servant. Let my light shine brightly for You. In Your name I pray, amen.

168—Small Group

As Bethany gathered the girls together, she asked us to turn to Titus 2:3–5, which allowed us to practice being a servant and apply the principle of salt and light in the most difficult setting—our homes.

Titus 2:3–5 instructs the older women to "admonish the young women to love their husbands, to love their children, to be discreet, chaste, homemakers, good, obedient to their own husbands, that the word of God will not be discredited." This passage means that the younger woman learns how to:

- Respect and honor those in authority over her.
- Build godly relationships.
- Be careful and wise in her decisions.
- Use time management skills in her home.
- Manage the family finances.
- Cook nutritious meals.
- Practice hospitality.
- Joyfully submit to her husband.
- Raise her children in the "fear and admonition of the Lord" (Ephesians 6:4) so that the Word of God will not be discredited or dishonored.

Miriam was quick to comment, "These verses don't really apply to us yet since we are not married." (She was the only one brave enough to verbalize what many of us were thinking!) Bethany smiled as she began her response, "You know, Miriam, I used to think the same thing until the godly woman who was discipling me shared that if I marry, nothing will change at the altar except my name and the legalization of my relationship with my groom.

"Everyday I am contributing some qualities to that future relationship, so if I don't respect my parents, love others, am not careful and wise in my actions, and don't fear the Lord then I will not have the strength of character to live according to this passage of Scripture when I am married. As well, if I live by crisis management, don't know basic life skills, am a poor manager of my money, know nothing about sound nutrition, can't cook, and know nothing about home management, then God's Word will be discredited in my home whether I am married or not. Just as I am an older woman to you, so you are an older woman to a junior high or elementary school girl. You can practice this Titus Two Principle now so that as you mature, God is always glorified in your home."

Continuing with her description Bethany shared that The MacArthur Study Bible provides a definition of the role of the older woman to the younger woman described in Titus 2:3-5 by stating, "their own example of godliness (v. 3) gives older women the right and the credibility to instruct younger women in the church. The obvious implication is that older women must exemplify the virtues (vs. 4, 5) that they 'admonish.'" The biblical rational for mentoring is clearly stated in Titus 2:5, "that the word of God may not be blasphemed." Dr. MacArthur writes. (Another word for blasphemed is dishonored.)

This is the purpose of godly conduct—to eliminate any reproach on Scripture. For a person to be convinced that God can save him or her from sin, that person needs to see someone who lives a holy life. When Christians claim to believe God's Word but don't obey it, the Word is dishonored. Many have mocked God and His truth because of the sinful behavior of those who claim to be Christians.

"Despite the fact that Titus 2:3-5 is an instruction, not a suggestion, few are willing to choose to be a servant by mentoring (teaching what she knows to another) a younger woman," Bethany concluded. "Excuses range from, 'I don't know that much' to 'no one cares what I have to say'; however, when an older woman hides behind these excuses she is sinning by failing to obey a clear instruction from her heavenly Father. Remembering that an excuse is not a substitute for obedience (1 Samuel 15:22), a WTIP joyfully practices this heavenly instruction!"

?4U

I used Pastor John's questions at the beginning of this chapter to evaluate my attitude toward servanthood. See here what I did, and maybe these kinds of choices can help you too.

I asked myself, what, if any, modifications need to be made to my life?

I set some personal goals that will either keep me functioning as a servant or help me become a servant.

I read Think Biblically! Recovering A Christian Worldview and used its contents to begin to develop my Christian Worldview. I plan to periodically review, evaluate, and expand it as I mature spiritually and academically.

For example, how does the principle of unselfish apply to what I learned in 168 these past weeks?

I will list practical ways that I can apply the principle of unselfish to my life. I will pray that my heavenly Father will motivate me to put the items on the list into action.

The principle of salt and light teaches me that a WTIP's presence should produce joy and blessing and at the same time offer a savoring and preserving influence in any environment.

I described the influence my presence has in a group environment.

I located verses that will challenge me to be a savoring and preserving influence.

I wrote some questions from the verses that should help me evaluate whether or not my influence in an environment is savory and preserving. Here is an example:
- Matthew 5:16—does my light shine in such a way that my heavenly Father is glorified by my works?

- I prayerfully made a list of my talents and abilities. I will investigate ministry opportunities in my church where I can use them. I will then contact the leadership in charge of the ministry and discuss becoming involved.

I studied Titus 2:3-5 and reread Dr. MacArthur's description of the passage. I then set personal goals that will help:
- respect my parents.
- love others.
- be careful and wise in my actions.
- fear the Lord.
- use time management skills in my daily responsibilities.
- manage my finances.
- cook nutritious meals.
- practice biblical hospitality.
- joyfully submit to those in authority over me.

I asked Bethany, a godly_older_woman, to hold me accountable as I strive, through our Lord's strength (Philippians 4:13), to reach the goals.

Through my Lord's strength, I will choose to be a servant by mentoring (teaching what she knows to another) a younger woman. I will begin this process by:
- Listing the skills and knowledge that I could share with a younger woman.
- Prayerfully committing the list to my heavenly Father and asking Him to make me excited about fulfilling His command to be a servant.
- Joyfully anticipating His "yes" answer to my prayer.
- As I spend time with a younger woman, I will be sure to follow Bethany's example and assure her that it's my privilege.

Study the life of Dorcas (Acts 9:36-42):

Describe the tasks she performed that proved she was unselfish. Think about how the tasks she completed affected her future.

IDK: LIFE SKILLS

Part 1

Are you a *smart worker* or is adrenalin your stimulant to accomplish your work?

Do you believe that God expects you to complete your assignments with *excellence*?

Do you know how to make sensible *decisions*?

Are you successful at managing your *resources*?

How do you set your *priorities*?

How do you use your *time*?

Tonight was the first 168 meeting for the new year. It doesn't seem possible the holidays are over, and we're ready to begin a new academic semester! And I get the opportunity to put into practice all that I've learned about life and living it to please God, especially this year. Pastor John began tonight's meeting with some probing questions that could affect our academic performance (I think some of our parents told him we use crisis management for the completion of our assignments.) This handout helped keep us focused.

Is Adrenalin Your Stimulant

Do you wait to begin an assignment at the last minute? When we do so, we are relying on adrenalin to be the stimulant that gives us the motivation to complete it. Our choice to do so places undue pressure on our time and energy, can create stress in our relationships, and can cause us to sin by having a bad attitude. Waiting until the last minute to work on a project is much like jumping out of a window of the tallest building in town and praying we won't get hurt.

—smart worker reminds me of Mrs. T's teaching on smart eating. My body will not be healthy without a sound nutritional plan, and my management skills will be deficient if I don't make an intentional effort to be a smart worker.

A *smart worker* is a person who:
- completes assignments with excellence
- makes sound decisions
- manages resources carefully

- sets realistic priorities
- uses time wisely

The next several sessions will guide you in becoming *smart workers*—not so that you will simply be model students, but so that your academic performance will bring glory to God (Colossians 3:17).

Some questions to help you evaluate your attitude toward excellence—
Do I:
- strive for quality?
- bring glory to God by being responsible (Ephesians 6:5)?
- persevere when quitting appears to be the logical choice (Philippians 3:13)?
- consistently work hard (Colossians 3:23; Galatians 6:2)?
- demonstrate loyalty (1 Corinthians 15:58)?
- project confidence (Philippians 4:13)?
- display graciousness (Proverbs 11:16)?
- rise above circumstances and choose to manifest a joyful outlook toward life (John 10:10)?

Keep the answers to these questions focused as we explore the topics for the next few weeks—making sensible decisions, managing our resources, setting our priorities, and using our time wisely.

Dear HF, I desire to be a smart worker rather than using adrenalin as my stimulant. Please help me do all of my assignments in a way that brings glory to You! In Your name I pray, amen.

IDK: LIFE SKILLS—Part II

FGI: For Girls Only!
Decisions are a constant factor in our lives. Decisions fall into three general categories:
Simple—those that require little thought such as "Do I want toast or cereal for breakfast?"
Basic—those only requiring a few minutes of concentrated thought like "Do I have the time to go out for a snack after high school group tonight?"
Important—decisions that will affect your life and perhaps the lives of others. Where to attend college would be an example of an *important decision*. The most *important decision* that we ever make is to become Christ's disciples (Luke 14:25–33).

The Six Cs *of Sensible Decision Making*

- Clearly defining the *decision* to be made. Writing down the *decision* helps me look at all of the circumstances that will affect the final *decision*.
- Committing the *decision* to my heavenly Father. Proverbs 3:5–6 and Proverbs 16:3 clearly state that I am to commit my way to the Lord and not lean on my own understanding.
- Collecting the information I need to make a sound *decision*. This research is to include both the facts and feelings involved.
- Considering the possible results or consequences of different options to my *decision*. For example, will the action I take affect others as well as myself?
- Confidently taking action on the *decision*. This may seem obvious, but many people go through the *decision-making process* and then fail to act on their plan. My *decision* has no strength until you act on it.
- Carefully evaluating the results of my *decision*. How did it turn out? I can learn from every *decision*—even the ones that turn out differently than I planned. Evaluating the results helps prepare me for your next *decision-making* opportunity.

Setting realistic *goals* moves me away from the crisis management that happens when adrenalin is my stimulant to accomplish my work.
By definition, a *goal* is simply a statement about what I want to accomplish. *Goals* should be stated in very specific terms so that I will know what *resources* I will need and what *priorities* must be established to

reach the *goals*. For example, if my *goal* is to earn a 4.0 for the semester, then I may need to study more and play less.

Bethany

(Next week: Manage our resources, set our priorities, and use our time effectively.)

Dear HF, thank You for guiding me to make sensible decisions so that I don't have to depend on adrenalin to accomplish my assignments. I ask that my goals and Your goals for my life would be the same. Help me to be careful to commit all of my decisions to You and to refuse to lean on my understanding. I do want my life to count for You. Please remind me to evaluate each of my decisions carefully before I move on to the next one. In Your name I pray, amen.

Tonight's 168 began with a discussion of how last week's questions had impacted our time-management decisions this week. Many of us shared that we had actually worked ahead on assignments rather than using adrenalin as our stimulant. We also commented that we enjoyed and benefitted from the assignments more by focusing on each of them bringing glory to our heavenly Father. Pastor John then introduced David and Abigail, both students at The Master's College. David is a senior Business major while Abbey, also a senior, is majoring in Home Economics—Family and Consumer Sciences with a Business concentration. Since they spend much time studying how to make decisions that will glorify God, he asked them to come and share with us some steps that can lead to wise decisions. Pastor John and David took the guys to another room while Abigail stayed in the high school room with the young women.

IDK: LIFE SKILLS—Part III

The 168 ladies eagerly gathered for Abby's next session. We were excited to share how last week's presentation had actually motivated us to move away from using adrenalin as our stimulant to accomplish our assignments. Before moving into the first topic of the evening, we also shared some of the goals we would like to accomplish this semester.

Notes from Managing My Resources

Good management begins with a plan that has specific steps to help me reach my goal. God made the earth before He created the animals and Adam (Genesis 1 and 2).

A workable plan requires that I:
- state my goals.
- identify the resources I have available
- outline the necessary steps to reach the goals.
- an inventory of my resources will reveal what I already have available to help reach them. It also shows what additional resources are necessary in order to make progress toward my goals.
- my inventory may include my time, money, available supplies, and personal skills. Once the resource inventory is complete, it's time to set my priorities.

Setting Priorities

If I'm going to become a smart worker, I must establish goals and priorities. The word priority means that some things come before or prior to some others—not instead of. Priorities help me to walk purposefully through life with guidelines for making sensible decisions.

Priorities also provide incentive (Proverbs 29:18) and allow me to use my resources and time wisely—not so that I am known as a time management expert but so that I am ultimately able to make a greater impact for the kingdom of God (Matthew 6:33-34).

As a Christian my priorities should reflect an eternal perspective and follow the model of the Lord, who glorified His Father while He was on earth by finishing the work His Father gave Him to do (John 17:4).

Priorities help me set goals. Proverbs 16:9 teaches that I should make plans, counting on God to direct me.

Proverbs 23:23 encourages me to get the facts and hold on tightly to all the good sense I can get.

Writing down my goals and the steps required to accomplish them helps me to visualize the tasks I need to do and put them in order of their priority.

Distinguish between the immediate and the urgent. There are many immediate but few urgent things.

The two things I need know about myself in order to effectively manage my resources are how my body cycles and my natural pace. Functioning within my body cycle allows me to maximize my most productive days and minimize my commitments on those days when my stamina is not as strong.

Some practical tips: Use blank calendar pages. Write on one tonight. The other is to be used as a master copy that can be duplicated—one page for each month of the year. Also look at look at word processing software to customize the page. Use colored highlighters and pencils to go through the Working Smarter Planning Process.

Step One—Organize
- Use one color to block out all of the time in class.
- Use one color to block out all other commitments (work, sports, ministry, etc).
- Use one color to designate all times available for study.
- Use one color to plan some time for fun, meals, etc.

Step Two—Analyze

- Begin by writing out Proverbs 29:18!

- Write out all known assignments for the semester on the master calendar.
- Daily or weekly add the additional assignments that must be completed.

Step Three—Strategize

- Divide all reading by the number of days you have to read the assigned pages.
- Put reading into scheduled time slots.
- Plan some time each week to work on large assignments.
- Check off assignments as they are completed

Step Four—Implement

- Begin each study session with prayer—Philippians 4:13.
- Exercise faith—Philippians 1:6.
- Adhere to a commitment to study daily. Abby shared that college students are expected to study 2 hours a day for each 1 hour of class attendance. She suggested that we ask each teacher how much time they expect us to spend daily on homework for that class.
- Graciously ask questions about your assignments. The teacher knows more about the assignment than your peers.
- Instead of listening to rumors about your potential teachers, wait until you actually have a class with them to form your thoughts about them. After all, you don't want them to have a negative attitude about you when they see your name on the class list. You owe the teachers the same courtesy.
- Maintain the basics—rest and sleep.
- Take class requirements one at a time. Remember that you don't need to complete the entire semester's work in one night.
- Use your absences carefully. Remember that school is preparation for life, not just a place to go when you don't have anything better to do.
- Choose to be considerate of both your teachers and classmates.

- Be EXCITED about what our Lord will teach you as you proceed through each class.

Take a jar, a bag of large colored gum balls, and a bag of popcorn from her backpack. The jar represents each WTIP. The colored gum balls are all of the things that should be a priority for a WTIP—prayer, Bible study, memorizing Scripture, meditating on Scripture, small group, 168. ministry, being a productive member of my family, and striving for excellence in my academics. The popcorn symbolizes all of the other tasks that are a part of my life—a job, sports, hanging out with friends, etc. Dump all of the popcorn in the bottom of the jar to demonstrate what happens when we get our priorities out of order and do our tasks first. Place the gum balls on top of the popcorn. It quickly becomes evident that the lid will not fit on the jar. Removing the gumballs and popcorn. place the gumballs in the jar first. add the popcorn. and the lid easily closes. When we choose to place our spiritual priorities ahead of our tasks. there is most always time for both..

<u>Collect the supplies and make a jar for my desk.</u>

Gracious hF, thank You for all of the practical tips I've learned about using my resources wisely. I know that it does not please You when I use adrenalin as the stimulant to complete my assignments. Help me to apply the tips to my life to that it reflects that I am a doer of the Word instead of simply a hearer. In Your name I pray, amen.

?4U

How does the principle of *prepared* apply to this learning?

List practical ways to apply the principle of *prepared* to life. Pray that God will motivate you to action.

What is the role of prayer in establishing priorities and goals? (See 1 Samuel 12:23; Daniel 9:16–19; Matthew 6:9–10; John 14:13–14; Ephesians 6:18; 1 Thessalonians 5:17; James 5:16; 1 John 5:15.)

In what ways has prayer influenced you? If your life is not been changed by prayer, why not?

In what ways are you presenting yourself as a living sacrifice, holy and acceptable to God? How can you renew your mind? (Romans 12:1–2)

Read Luke 9:57–62.

What were the predetermined *priorities* of these three men?

How did their *priorities* determine their answers to Jesus' call?

How do your personal *priorities* determine your answer to my Master's requests?

Do I have a "not now, Jesus, because . . ." answer?

What will I do to change this situation?

Using Luke 14:25–33, I wrote my testimony that describes the most *important decision* that I ever made—choosing to become one of Christ's disciples.

That *decision* affects the daily *decisions* I make in the following ways:
• I used the following verses, to write a description of my salvation experience.
  Romans 3:10.
  Romans 3:23.
  Romans 5:8.

Romans 5:12.
Romans 6:23.
Romans 10:9.
Romans 10:10.
Romans 10:13.

- I memorized the order of the verses and become familiar with their content so that I can confidently share with someone else how to become one of Christ's disciples.
- I started using the WORKING SMARTER PLANNING PROCESS to manage my *resources*.
- I collected the supplies and created my own *Resource Management Jar* and placed it on my desk so that I am reminded daily to keep my *priorities* in the right order.
- I studied the life of Elizabeth (Luke 1:5–20, 24–25) and
- Described her reactions to the change in her lifestyle that proved she was prepared.
- Recorded how the tasks she completed affected her future
- I also studied the life of Job's wife (Job 1:1–3, 6–12, 2:1–10, 42:10–13) and
- Described her reactions to the change in her lifestyle that proved she was not prepared.
- Recorded how the tasks she completed affected her future.

TBD: Style

Is the Label True? 168 began tonight with an interesting activity. Pastor John had the guys sit in the first rows of chairs. He indicated that he was going to show slides of trendy girls' clothes. He asked the guys to state the first thoughts that crossed their minds as the slides were displayed on the screen. It was a good thing that the girls were seated behind the guys because some of the comments were pretty embarrassing for us to hear and some of our faces blushed.

When the final slide was completed Pastor John held up a large can of peas (at least that is what the label read) and asked what was in the can. Several of the guys took the opportunity to sarcastically state that the contents were obvious—the label indicated that peas were inside. "You think so?" Pastor John responded. He then proceeded to dump the contents into a glass bowl. Much to our surprise green beans poured into the bowl. The label on the can was not true.

This illustration was followed by a great explanation! "When I grocery shop, one of the items I first look at is the label to determine that I am purchasing the product that best meets my need. As a consumer, I expect the label to provide accurate information about the nutritional value, serving sizes, and perhaps how to prepare the product so I will get the best results from using it. I also know that the United States government requires accurate labeling on products produced in America. I would be upset if I purchased a product whose label informed me that the package contained the item described only to find, upon opening it, that it contained a different product! While my demonstration was entertaining if it happened in real life I would be upset." He then explained that his wife had carefully removed a label from a pea can and glued it to the green bean can to provide him with the visual example.

The slides and the demonstration were the introduction to this evening's study. Clothing, is a visual description of our character, just as a product's label explains its anticipated performance. As God's children, we are to be careful to groom our character and our bodies so that our inward and outward beauty complements one another. Keeping this thought in mind will help us practice the truth of 1 Peter 3:3-4 that teaches "Do not let your adorning be external—the braiding of hair, the wearing of gold, or the putting on of clothing—but let your adorning be the hidden person of the heart with the imperishable beauty of a gentle and quiet spirit, which in God's sight is very precious." This Scripture applies to both guys and girls.

Just as the United States government requires all clothing and fabric manufactures to put accurate labels on their products, so God's Word challenges us to dress in such a way that our outward appearance accurately reflects our character. Mark 10:19 says that failure to do so sends a conflicting message to others. He then challenged us with a spiritual grooming activity. We are to record how much time we spend on our spiritual grooming on an average day and then to spend only that amount of time on their physical grooming the following day. He then asked us to consider the question, "what do you think your grooming for the day will look like on the day complete my project?" He suggested we select a Saturday to complete it just in case our spiritual grooming time is not very long.

168 Notes: The "M" Word

Modesty is a word that we don't hear very often anymore—and when we do, it's often thought of it as behavior that our parents choose to adopt once they have had all of their fun.

By definition *modesty* means "having or showing regard for the decencies of behavior, speech and dress."

We all sighed when he transitioned to his next point—modesty. Sensing our displeasure, he quickly moved into his discussion of the "M" word.

Spiritually, *modesty* is an issue of the heart ♥—if our thoughts are focused on the attributes found in Philippians 4: 8–9, then more than likely our external appearance will be modest.

When he tied Scripture to the "M" word we began to think that it could possibly apply to teenagers too. A second ?: "Is modesty an absolute or outdated standard for the twenty-first-century Christian teen?"
We all wanted to shake our heads "no," but Pastor John's serious expression indicated that probably would not be a good idea.
The immutability (changelessness) of God would be in question if the Scriptures that give us a standard for dress are not applicable for today. A final question, "If we think God has changed His mind about one passage of Scripture, how can we be sure that He has not changed His mind about others?"

Discussion Group Instructions
We were divided into groups, asked to read several Scriptures that talk about modesty, and write down the instructions they give. After discussing the verses as a group, we wrote personalized standards.

Dear hF, thank You for the lesson about truth in labeling. I truly want my outward appearance to be pleasing to You. Please give me the wisdom to know how to choose clothes so that my inward and outward beauty complement one another. Help me focus on the attributes found in Philippians 4: 8–9 so my external appearance will be modest. In Your name I pray, amen.

Sometimes my hF answers my prayers really quickly. Today was one of those occasions. First period was an all school assembly. Mr. Solomon's topic was about the campus dress code. The body language of the students reflected that they were not excited about the subject. I wondered if he and Pastor John had consulted with one another.
He began by affirming that many students comply with the dress code but indicated that there are an increased number of infractions. He then used a PowerPoint presentation to refresh our memories on the code's content that is distributed by the County Office of Education. First period teachers passed out a copy to each student.

Students of West Ranch High School are expected to dress in a manner that is supportive of a positive learning environment that is free of distractions and disruptions. There is a direct correlation between student dress and student behavior. Students will be expected to observe modes of dress, styles of hair, and personal grooming, which support the learning environment. The purpose of this dress code is to assure that consistency and interpretation is implemented county-wide, thus providing equitable treatment for all students.

A general statement followed the display of the code. "Any clothing that is viewed as distracting because of extremes in style, fit, color, pattern, fabric, etc., shall not be permitted." Mr. Solomon then listed specific clothing that could not be worn on campus and reminded the teachers that he expected them to enforce the school dress code. A solemn student body filed out of the multi-purpose room because a number of students were wearing clothing that violated the dress code.

Right after assembly, I went to Mrs. T.'s class after the assembly before leaving for work. The new topic Mrs. Titus introduced reflected that she knew before the assembly what Mr. Solomon was going to talk about. One of the things I really like about Mrs. Titus is that she does not focus on the negative—what students can't do. Instead, she suggested that her students could become the leaders in illustrating to the students of West Ranch High how they could be trendy and still comply with the dress code. Our topic for the next several weeks is "Clothing Selection." We are going to learn how to use the line and design principles to dress along with other information that will help us become good consumers of our clothing dollars.

Clothing Selection Topic #1—THE EMOTIONAL EFFECT OF LINES

Facts About Lines

The shape of a <u>garment</u> is created by <u>design</u> lines. The actual shape of the garment has a lot to do with your shape. Lines create the <u>mood</u> of the garment. They are either <u>straight</u> or <u>curved.</u>

Straight lines tend to look <u>formal.</u> severe and business-like. Curved lines suggest <u>delicacy</u> and <u>softness</u>. They can make a person appear rounder. friendlier. and less formal.

Lines can be used for both <u>structure</u> and <u>decoration</u> in a garment. Structural lines are created by <u>seams</u> and <u>darts</u>—the construction that holds the garment together and creates the fit. A skirt. for example. can be straight. A-line. very full or very tight. A jacket could have a diagonal line or a zipper down the front. Ribbon. lace. and trim that are added to a garment provide decorative lines. Pockets. collars. and lapels create edge lines.

Whether the line is <u>structural.</u> <u>decorative.</u> or <u>edge</u> the design <u>principle</u> is the same—the eye stops where the line stops.

A square neckline can make a round face appear more oval. a curved neckline softens a square face. while a V-shape neckline can be used to make a round face look slimmer.

Instructions from Mrs. T.:

As a group evaluate some of the garments listed in the school dress code as inappropriate with the statement "the eye stops where the line stops."

Create your own "Emotional Effect of Lines" Chart.

<u>Group Discussion Highlights</u>

Tight clothing outlines the body and often draws attention to parts that are private.

Tops that expose the waist. hips. or midriff cause the eye to stop at that part of the body. This can be a distraction to both the guys and male faculty members.

Low necklines cause the eyes to focus on the bust line. This too can be a distraction to men of all ages.

THE EMOTIONAL EFFECT OF LINES

Horizontal lines carry the eye across the figure, making it appear shorter and wider.

Vertical lines add apparent height. They make a person look taller and slimmer.

Sharp Angles add interest but in excess they are displeasing.

Sunburst lines add height when used on hats. They are slenderizing and graceful in pleated skirts.

V-shaped lines are brought to a point, forming a V. These lines in clothes are slenderizing unless they are too wide or flattened out, in which case they broaden the figure.

Down sweeping lines are sad and can cause the wearer to look tired and depressed.

Upswing lines are buyout and soften an angular structure of face or figure.

Curved lines are graceful and flattering to the figure. They suggest softness and easiness.

Diagonal lines make a person look either slimmer or heavier, depending on whether the line is more vertical or horizontal.

Broken lines run perpendicular to one another. Broken lines shorten the length of long, straight lines.

When a woman allows the line to stop at a private part of her body. she is allowing men to view areas not meant for their eyes.

Clothing Selection Topic #3—A Touch of Color

Having established the importance of line in our clothing selections today we moved to the importance of color in our wardrobe. Mrs. T. began the study with some basic color facts: Color can affect the way I feel. It can also affect the ways others react to me. Some colors can make me happy while others can put me in a sad mood.

Color also affects the way I look. It can make me appear larger or smaller, healthy or unhealthy, and even happy or unhappy.

Color can change the look of my skin. It can also change the look of other colors I wear. Mrs. T. demonstrated this by showing us a piece of red fabric and a piece of blue fabric. She then placed the pieces of fabric next to one another. Both colors looked slightly different from the way they looked alone. Working as partners, we then spent some time evaluating what color does for our skin appearance. Using color collars cut from pieces of red, yellow, blue, green, orange, and purple (violet) fabric we completed this chart:

COLOR	WHAT DOES THE COLOR DO FOR YOUR SKIN APPEARANCE?
Red	
Yellow	
Blue	
Green	
Orange	
Purple	

→ Note homework assignment!
Bring a copy of a color wheel on a notebook sized sheet of paper for tomorrow's class.

(Mrs. Titus began class today by asking each student to display her color wheel.)
Effective color combinations:
- please the wearer.
- look nice on the wearer.
- create a pleasant over-all effect with the figure and skin.
- are appropriate to the occasion and the place.
- have variety and interest.

What do I want color to do?"—some basic questions:
- Does the color look flattering on me?
- Am I happy in my color combinations?
- Do others compliment my color combinations?
- Are my color combinations becoming to my hair, skin, eyes, and size?
- Do my color combinations emphasize my best features and camouflage the less attractive ones?
- What colors should I combine, and how many colors should I use?
- When and where will I wear the outfit I am coordinating?
- What idea or mood do I wish to create?
- How simple or elaborate are the other items—such as jewelry and trim—that will be used?

Mrs. T's Concluding Comments
As the class period concluded, Mrs. Titus complimented us on the helpful decision-making questions we developed and shared that tomorrow we would look at some strategies that can help us build wardrobes that we really use instead of giving storage space to garments we only wear once in a while.

Clothing Selection Topic #4—Building Your Wardrobe

Wardrobe building questions:
Would you rather have a closet and chest filled with clothes you really wear, or use your storage space with garments you only wear once in a while?

Think about the clothes hanging in your closet today. Which ones do you wear most often?
What characteristics do these clothes have?

Clothes that I really enjoy wearing usually have three things in common:
- I like wearing them.
- I can wear them for different kinds of activities.
- they look good with a lot of my other clothes—I can mix and match them.

Wardrobe Building

Most teens enjoy getting and wearing new clothes. Making a decision about what to buy can be difficult—especially if you would like to purchase a garment that all of your friends are wearing but know that it does not look good on you.

Making Wise Clothing Decisions

Step One—Make Your Clothing Decisions
When I shop, I make specific decisions based on these questions:
- What type of garment do I <u>need</u>?_____
- How do I want the garment to <u>fit</u>? _____
- What kind of <u>quality</u> do I want for this garment?_____
- What kind of <u>upkeep</u> does the garment need (dry cleaning, regular pressing, etc.)?_____
- What <u>information</u> does the garment tags and care <u>labels</u> give me about the garment? _____

Step Two—Determine Your Clothing Needs
Building a <u>practical</u> wardrobe for my lifestyle requires that I make a <u>list</u> of the kind of clothes I need. Some questions I need to think about are:
- Do I need <u>special</u> clothes for different <u>seasons</u> such as a heavy coat for winter?
- What <u>type</u> of clothing is acceptable according to the school dress <u>code</u>?
- What <u>activities</u> do I participate in that require <u>specialized</u> clothing (sports, a job, exercising, etc.)?
- Do I have a <u>need</u> for special occasion or <u>dressy</u> clothes?
- What kind of clothes do I usually <u>choose</u> to wear?

Step Three—Take a Clothing Inventory
The clothing inventory is simply a list of clothes that I now have stored in my closet and drawers. To complete the inventory I need to:
→ Sort the clothing into five categories—the clothes I:
  - like and wear <u>often</u>.

- need to <u>repair</u>.
- don't wear very often.
- have that don't mix or match well with anything else I own.
- have <u>outgrown</u> or worn out.

→ Return the clothes I like and wear to my closet and drawers. As I do, I need to list the garments on this chart:

Wardrobe Planning Chart									
Garment	School	Casual	Work	Dressy	OK	Repair Alter or Discard	Need	Approx Cost	Plan
Pants and jeans									
Skirts									
Sweaters									
Shirts									
Jackets									
Accessories									

As I complete the chart I can <u>check</u> each box that applies to the garment. since I use most of my garments for more than one type of activity.

- Check for <u>blank</u> spots on the chart.
- Plan to give <u>attention</u> to any garments checked in the repair or alter pile.
- <u>Discard</u> the garments I have outgrown or won't wear again.
- <u>Evaluate</u> the chart to decide if:
    I have too much of one <u>type</u> of clothing.
    there are <u>categories</u> for which I have nothing at all.
    there are <u>new</u> uses for garments that I thought had only <u>one</u> purpose.
    there are garments in the <u>do-not-wear</u> pile that might work for another <u>purpose</u>.
- Fill in the <u>gaps</u>. The blanks spaces on the inventory tell me what kind of <u>new</u> clothing I might need. Before going shopping, I need to create a <u>buying</u> plan to make sure that what I purchase will work with my <u>current</u> wardrobe.

Step Four—Create a Buying Plan

When creating my *Buying Plan* I should consider:

- the <u>colors</u> of the garments I need.
- the fabric <u>weight</u>.
- <u>consult</u> my parents about my wardrobe plan and how <u>much</u> money I can spend.
- <u>decide</u> on how much I can spend on each <u>garment</u>.
- concentrate the <u>largest</u> amount of money toward the garments I will wear the <u>most</u>.
- avoid <u>buying</u> garments or accessories that are not in my plan. A fad item, or something I will only wear several times, can be a <u>waste</u> of money.
- if my <u>budget</u> will not allow for everything I think I need, I should buy the garments that I can most use <u>now</u>. I can delay buying the other items until they are on sale or next <u>season</u>.

As I wrote my journal entry this evening, I was reminded of how much the information we learned matched some biblical principles found in the Bible.

Proverbs 14:1 teaches me that a wise woman builds her house. 1 Corinthians 14:40 reminds me that I am to do my tasks in an orderly fashion.

Luke 16:10 promises that if I learn to be faithful in small things, I will be faithful if my resources increase.

Philippians 4:11 challenges me to learn to be content with what I have.

Dear HF, thank You for providing my parents with the ability to provide for my clothing needs. I ask to have a teachable spirit to work with Mom to build a wardrobe that pleases You and reflects good choices. Please help me to be content with all You have provided and to carefully care for all of my garments. In Your name I pray, amen.

Clothing Selection Topic # 5—Clothing Care

Today Mrs. T. gave us the opportunity to focus on the care of our clothing and began with a fun lab experience. The topic was stains, and she introduced it by reminding us that spills and spots should be taken care of as soon as they happen whenever possible. The longer stains are left in a garment the more challenging they are to remove. Some spills or spots like juice, blood, or perspiration can permanently stain some fabrics. Stains can also weaken the fiber.

STAIN REMOVAL LAB

Lab Introduction
- This lab experience involves removing stains from fabrics.
- You have pieces of fabric that have common stains on them.
- Work with a partner to remove the stains following the demonstrated procedures.
- Record the stain treatments listed on the instruction sheet on the Stain Removal Chart.
- Word-process and submit tomorrow. → Note homework assignment!

Lab Demonstration
- The removal of two of the stains, blood and perspiration, was demonstrated.
- The most important procedure to follow is to work from the wrong side of the stain.
- Working from the wrong side of stain allows it to leave the fabric the way that it entered instead of forcing the stain through all of the fibers
- Remember basic laundering procedures:
    Read care labels.
    Sort clothes before laundering.
    Treat spots, stains, and very dirty areas.
    If machine washing, use the recommended amount of detergent and bleach type (chlorine and nonchlorine), if necessary.
    Use the appropriate water temperature.
    Don't overload the washer with clothes.
    Dry clothes according to the label instructions.
    Press or iron if necessary.

Stain Removal Chart

STAIN	TREATMENT
Blood	Soak the fabric in cold water as soon as possible. Make a paste from detergent. Place detergent paste on the *wrong* side of the fabric. Rub gently until the stain is removed. Rinse with cold water. If necessary, launder according to garment directions. Remember that hot water will make the stain permanent.
Gum	Harden the gum by rubbing it with ice. Scrape off as much as possible with a *dull* knife. Make a paste from detergent. Place detergent paste on the *wrong* side of the fabric. Rub gently until the stain is removed. Rinse with cold water. If necessary, launder according to garment directions.
Chocolate and Cocoa	Soak in cold water. Make a paste from detergent. Place detergent paste on the *wrong* side of the fabric. Rub gently until the stain is removed. Rinse with cold water. If necessary, launder according to garment directions.
Coffee or Tea	Spray the *wrong* side of the stain with pre-soak product or diluted nonchlorine bleach. Use the hottest water that is safe for the fabric. Rinse with cold water. If necessary, launder according to garment directions.
Cosmetics (Makeup)	Make a paste from detergent or use undiluted, liquid detergent. Place liquid or detergent paste on the *wrong* side of the fabric. Rub gently until the stain is removed. Rinse with cold water. A second application may be needed. If necessary, launder according to garment directions.

STAIN	TREATMENT
Grass and Foliage	Make a paste from detergent. Place detergent paste on the *wrong* side of the fabric. Rub gently until the stain is removed. Use a mild nonchlorine or chlorine bleach if stain is not removed with the detergent paste. Rinse with cold water. If necessary, launder according to garment directions.
Grease and Oil	Scrape off as much grease as possible with a *dull* knife. Make a paste from detergent using warm water. Place detergent paste on the *wrong* side of the fabric. Rub gently until the stain is removed. Rinse with cold water. If necessary, launder according to garment directions.
Ink (ball point)	Rub white petroleum jelly (Vaseline) on the *wrong* side of the fabric. Make a paste from detergent. Place detergent paste on the *wrong* side of the fabric. Use a mild nonchlorine or chlorine bleach if stain is not removed with the detergent paste. Rub gently until the stain is removed. Rinse with cold water. If necessary, launder according to garment directions,
Perspiration	Make a paste from detergent. Place detergent paste on the *wrong* side of the fabric. Rub gently until the stain is removed. Rinse with cold water. If stain remains, use a tooth brush to apply a small amount of household ammonia to a new stain. If the stain is old use a tooth brush to apply a small amount of white vinegar. If necessary, launder according to garment directions.
Soda (soft drinks)	Gently rub the spot from the *wrong* side of the fabric immediately. Rinse with cold water. If necessary, launder according to garment directions.

As I word-processed my chart this evening I was reminded of how much sin is like the stains we worked with today. Stains can permanently damage a garment if not treated immediately. Likewise, unconfessed sin can seriously affect my spiritual life. Just as it's important to work from the wrong side of the stain to completely remove it, so I am to have my heart cleansed rather than just trying to change my outward behavior (Psalm 51). I am thankful that 1 John 1:9, "If we confess our sins, He is faithful and just to forgive us of sin and to cleanse us from all unrighteousness," provides the stain removal instructions for sin.

During my quiet time I thought I would try and match the basic laundering procedures with the process for cleansing my spiritual life. I recorded my thoughts in this chart:

Laundry Procedure	Spiritual Application
Read care labels.	Consistently study God's Word (Psalm 119:11)
Sort clothes before laundering.	Be willing to separate myself from sinful habits (2 Corinthians 6:17).
Treat spots, stains, and very dirty areas.	Be quick to confess sin and turn away from the behavior (1 John 1:9).
If machine washing, use the recommended amount of detergent and bleach, if necessary.	Ask my heavenly Father to use whatever is necessary to cleanse me from sin (Psalm 51:7).
Use the appropriate water temperature.	I am to be filled with spiritual zeal; I am not lukewarm as were the members of the church of Laodicea (Revelation 3:15).
Don't overload the washer with clothes.	Be careful to not overload my schedule so that I don't have time to spend with my heavenly Father (Luke 10:38–42).
Dry clothes according to the label instructions.	Graciously accept the refining process my heavenly Father uses in my life (Malachi 3:2–3).

Laundry Procedure	Spiritual Application
Press or iron if necessary	Recognize that the heat of trials strengthens my character (James 1:2–4).

Dear hF, the lessons about stain removal remind me that I need to be as quick to remove sin from my life. Thank You that You Word provides the formula for sin's removal. I don't want my life ruined because I failed to confess and forsake my sin. In Your name I pray, amen.

Tips to Making the Label True.

I was excited to meet with Bethany tonight to get her input into all I am learning about modesty and clothing selection. I knew that she would be a good resource because she is taking a class in Clothing Selection as a part of her Home Economics major. Once we ordered our dinner (tonight was our "girls' night out") and caught up on life, I shared with her what I was learning about modesty and clothing selection. She started laughing when I asked her, "Do I have to look old-fashioned to dress modestly?" She began her response from a biblical point of view.

"King Solomon, who knew many beautifully dressed women, answers your question in fourteen words: 'Like a gold ring in a pig's snout is a beautiful woman without discretion' (Proverbs 11:22)". Since I had already studied this verse I knew the definition of discretion.

Bethany then suggested that we focus on some tips for dressing that makes dressing modestly practical:

· *Your face displays your character.* Proverbs 15:13 teaches us that a "joyful heart makes a cheerful face." You can draw attention to your face by selecting necklines that complement it. For example, the shape of a collar or bow allows the eye to linger on the face.

- Test your garments for wearability. Do this by positioning yourself in front of a mirror to observe what others will see.
- Bend over to check how revealing your neckline is.
- Sit down and cross your legs to check the length of shorts and skirts.
- Bend over to see how far your skirt moves up.
- Take a large step to examine skirt slits.
- Place your hands above your head to see how much of the midriff is exposed.
- Take the "Truth in Packaging Inventory."
- Your clothing is a label for your character. What does it communicate about you?
- What values determine the clothing you wear?
- When you select your clothing, what are your first thoughts?
- When you dress for the day, who are you thinking about pleasing?
- What is your response to the question "Is modesty an absolute or obsolete value for the twenty-first-century Christian woman?"

We had a great time discussing each of the tips she suggested. As we finished our dinner, Bethany commented, "Customs of dress change with the seasons, and fashions are as changeable as the wind. Any woman who puts her hopes in these to make herself look beautiful will find her standards of beauty constantly changing. A WTIP directs her energy on her character first and her physical appearance second. This woman, no matter what her age, will ensure that her beauty will last."

Heavenly Father, please help me to want to follow Peter's instruction of not allowing my beauty to be all on the outside. I ask that you give me the desire to daily groom myself spiritually because Your Word tells me that this attitude pleases You (1 Peter 3:3-4)!

?4U

I studied Deuteronomy 22:5, Proverbs 11:22, Proverbs 31:21-25, Romans 12:1-2, and 1 Timothy 2:9-10 then wrote my personal modesty standards.

I defined how the principle of honorable applies to what I learned in this assignment.

I listed practical ways that I can apply the principle of honorable to my life. I am praying that my hF will motivate me to put the items on the list into action.

I applied the Tips to Making the Label True to my clothing selections by asking these questions:

• What choices am I making that show that I dress as a daughter of royalty?

• What changes need to be made to insure that my clothing choices are a true label of my royal heritage?

I used the following chart to develop my understanding of how my hF wants me to groom my character:

Daily I Will . . .	Verse Action
1 Peter 5:5	Clothe myself with humility.
Deuteronomy 6:8	
Proverbs 31:25	
Romans 13:14	
Colossians 3:12	
Colossians 3:14	
Galatians 3:26	
Colossians 3:10	
Ephesians 4:24	
Ephesians 6:11-17	
Proverbs 1:8-9	
1 Peter 3:4	

Use the The Emotional Effect of Lines chart and the statement "the eye stops where the line stops" to evaluate my clothing choices. I use this information to dress trendy and, at the same time, maintain the dress codes established by my parents, church, and school.

I analyzed how the lines on a garment affect the overall impression it makes.

I evaluated how the necklines on a garment can change the way people see my body or face shape.

I completed this color chart for myself:

COLOR	WHAT DOES THE COLOR DO FOR MY SKIN APPEARANCE
Red	
Yellow	
Blue	
Green	
Orange	
Purple	

I located a color wheel and refer to it as I make clothing selections.

I prayed about what I might you do with clothing I never wear that will assist those less fortunate than me and

Prepared the clothing to give to them so it would best reflect God's love.

Located the contact agencies that could use my clothing to minister to others. I contacted them and offered my services in laundering and repairing the donated clothing.

I studied the life of Sarah (Genesis 18:1-5, 21:1-13; Hebrews 11:1 1 Peter 3:6) and

Described the tasks she performed that proved she was honorable. Thought about how the task she completed affected her future

I studied the life of Mary (Luke 1:26-38) and

Described the tasks she performed that proved she was honorable. Meditated on how the tasks she completed affected her future.

TTYL

<u>Happened in 168.</u> As we met for high school group tonight Pastor John began by telling us that he is concerned about the way we speak to and about one another. He is also disappointed in the way we talk about others. I have to admit that at times we all tease too hard and say things that are not very kind. Though we always end the statement with, "just kidding," the reality is that there is probably always some truth in our teasing words. He confronted us with the thought that our speech was not a very good example of our faith to weak Christians or unbelievers. I was convicted about my words as he asked us to consider thinking about five questions before we open our mouths. He found them in <u>Becoming a Woman Who Pleases God</u>.

Is it kind?

Is it true?

Is it necessary?

Is it gossip (sharing private information with those who are not a part of the situation)?

Am I practicing good listening, paying attention?

Since I want my speech to reflect that my Lord has control of my tongue and because I could not give positive answers to all of the questions, I was definitely ready to listen to the evening's teaching. He continued by asking the question that was the title of our handout for the evening.

168 Floss your mouth!

Since we're teenagers, you can imagine the verbal and nonverbal responses Pastor John received from that question! He ignored our responses by giving us a bit of a physiology lesson.

<u>Physically,</u> the tongue is one of the body's most versatile parts of the body.

The Tongue . . .
- plays an important role in <u>speaking</u> and in <u>eating</u>.
- is the bearer of <u>taste</u> and <u>tactile</u> (touch) sensations.
- gives us <u>pleasure</u> in eating.
- gives <u>warning</u> of possible injury by registering <u>pain</u> when foods are too hot and <u>revulsion</u> (distaste) when they are <u>spoiled</u>.
- in its role as <u>manipulator</u>, it takes food into the mouth, <u>moves</u> it between the upper and lower <u>teeth</u> for chewing, and then <u>molds</u> the crushed and moistened particles into a ball for swallowing.

(Since everyone was beginning to react to this description, he quickly moved on to the important part of the lesson.)

Spiritually, <u>James 3:3–5</u> teaches that even though the tongue is <u>small</u>, it has the <u>power</u> to <u>control</u> everything in our lives. Isaiah 6:1–8 relates the account of how God called <u>Isaiah</u> to become a prophet. He did so by <u>first</u> giving Isaiah a vision of His <u>awesome</u> holiness and then by <u>purifying</u> the prophet's <u>tongue</u>. Isaiah realized, after catching a glimpse of God's holiness that his tongue needed to be <u>cleansed</u> (6:5–8).

Cleansing the WTIP Tongue

How clean is your tongue—or have you never really considered your tongue in terms of its cleanliness? You normally don't...

- check it in the mirror multiple times during the day unless you are sick.
- go on shopping trips for it.
- schedule appointments for it at the tongue groomer.
- purchase grooming aids for it. It's the tongue, more than the <u>shape</u> of your <u>face</u> or the <u>dimensions</u> of your figure or your <u>theological</u> knowledge, which determines your attractiveness. Your <u>reputation</u> will, in large part, be established by the <u>use</u> you make of your tongue. It leaves a <u>lasting</u> impression on people (Proverbs 12:25, 15:25, 25:11).

The tongue <u>labels</u> your character. The bystanders at the <u>trial</u> of Jesus identified <u>Peter</u> as a <u>follower</u> of Christ by his <u>speech</u> (Matthew 26:73).

Your tongue is a reflection of what is in your <u>heart</u> (Luke 6:45).

It's no easy task to cleanse your tongue—James 3:7–12 tells us that no <u>human</u> can <u>tame</u> their own tongue—only God can do this (Acts 2:1–11). It takes walking in God's Speaking Spa and allowing His Spirit to cleanse and tone our tongue into a useful <u>instrument</u> for His glory.

Our own effort is also necessary. We must <u>want</u> to have a cleansed tongue.

Our heavenly Father requires that we use the wealth of <u>grooming</u> instructions in His <u>Word</u> to help with the process. We were then introduced to some of the services at God's Tongue <u>Grooming</u> Spa, beginning with the Tongue Grooming Baseline Chart.

A Grooming Consultation for the Tongue

Instructions:
1. When we begin an exercise program, a set of baseline measurements are helpful. The same is true with Tongue Grooming.
2. Working as partners, collect baseline measurements for your tongue.

3. Complete the Tongue Grooming Baseline Chart

Tongue Grooming Baseline Chart	
Category	**Measurement**
Approximate length of my tongue	
My height in inches	
Percentage of my height that is tongue: Tongue length divided by Height = _____or _____% (My tongue length is 2.5" and my height is height is 66" $\frac{2.5}{66}$ = .03 or 3%	

4. Once the measurements are completed ask yourself the question, "Am I going to allow something that is _____% (insert your calculation) of my body height control me?" (The group was pretty quiet as we thought about our responses.)
5. Spend some time talking to your heavenly Father about your tongues.
6. During the week complete "A Speaking Spa" for next week's 168 meeting.

Dear hF, thank You for this series on talking. I do want my words to encourage others. I also want them to reflect that I am Your daughter. Please help me to complete the homework honestly and be willing to take advantage of some of the services at the Speaking Spa. In Your name I pray, amen.

Say What?

Place the number that best reflects your response to the statement in the space provided.

_____1. I have a challenge controlling my tongue
   5 = never; 4 = very seldom; 3 = seldom; 2 = sometimes;
   1 = usually; 0 = regularly

_____2. After an argument, I usually feel that I was most hurt by
   2 = the issues that were involved; 1 = the words that were said.

_____3. In relation to gossip, I feel that I am 4 = never; 3 = seldom;
   2 = sometimes; 1 = frequently guilty.

_____4. During this past week I chose to use my tongue constructively to
   1 = comfort a friend; 1 = express love to my parents;
   1 = encourage a teacher; 1 = express sympathy or concern;
   1 = witness for Christ.*

_____5. Generally, I believe I talk about
   3 = the right amount; 2 = too little; 1 = too much

_____6. The misuses of the tongue I have under control include
   1 = too talkative; 1 = complaining; 1 = gossiping;
   1 = lying; 1 = exaggerating; 1 = boastful; 1 = too loud.*

_____7. The qualities of the biblical use of the tongue that I have culti-
   vated are
   1 = kind; 1 = affirming; 1 = contented.*

_____8. I have an appreciative tongue
   4 = frequently; 3 = sometimes; 2 = seldom; 1 = never.

_____9. I practice the Ecclesiastes "a time to" passage and know when
   to keep silent and when to speak
   4 = frequently; 3 = sometimes; 2 = seldom; 1 = never.

_____10. I choose to gossip
   4 = never; 3 = seldom; 2 = sometimes; 1 = frequently.

_____ Consultation Total

*Your number is the sum of all of the items that apply to you.

See Grooming Consultation for My Tongue Interpretation in ?4U

This is absolutely amazing!

God's Tongue GROOMING Spa Menu

A somber group met for high school group this evening. Most of us had completed "A Grooming Consultation for My Tongue" and found that our tongues are not very beautiful. Pastor John prayed and then began our time together by stating that once our "Tongue Grooming Baseline Chart" is completed we need to select the order of our Tongue Grooming regiment from God's Tongue Grooming Spa Menu. There are four to choose from—the Appreciative Regiment, the Quiet Regiment, the Affirming Regiment, and the Contented Regiment. With humble hearts we were ready to learn about the details of the regiments.

The Appreciative Regiment
One of the most evident signs of genuine godliness is a sincere display of appreciation for your heavenly Father's work in your life.

What, according to Romans 1:21-27, is the terrible fault of those who have drifted away from God? The root cause is thanklessness. God's most influential were appreciative people: David dedicated many of his Psalms to the theme of thankfulness (Psalm 35, 65, 92, 108, and 116). David always directed the giving of thanks to the will and not the emotions. That means we are to give thanks because it's the right thing to do—even if we don't feel like it.

Paul began most of his letters with a statement of thanks (Romans 1:8; 1 Corinthians 1:4; Ephesians 1:15-16).

Paul, in his letters, chose specific individuals, such as Priscilla and Aquila (Romans 16:3-4) and Onesiphorus (2 Timothy 1:16-18), for special words of appreciation. (write notes to Mrs. T, Pastor John, and Bethany.)

Meditate for a moment on the account of the ten lepers healed by Jesus (Luke 17:11-19). Nine went on their way without saying thank you. The one with an appreciative tongue returned to give thanks and received an additional blessing. Not only did he experience physical healing, but he had the opportunity to become personally acquainted with The Healer!

An appreciative tongue changes your <u>perspective</u> on things. Think about the <u>difference</u> between a <u>vulture</u> and a <u>hummingbird</u>. The vulture will find a <u>decaying</u> dead body, because that's what it is <u>looking</u> for. The hummingbird will find a beautiful flower, because that's what it is looking for. Reality is you will <u>find</u> what you want to find! Are you a vulture or a hummingbird?

Dear Heavenly Father, please cleanse my speech so it's like that of the hummingbird rather than a vulture!

The Quiet Regimen

The Bible certainly is not <u>silent</u> about the <u>art</u> of keeping silent:

Proverbs 10:19 states, "In the <u>multitude</u> of words, <u>sin</u> is not <u>lacking</u>. But he who <u>restrains</u> his lips is <u>wise</u>." Ecclesiastes says, in the well-known "a time to" passage, that there is "a time to <u>keep</u> silence, and a <u>time</u> to speak" (3:7).

Psalm 4:4 teaches us to "<u>meditate</u> within your heart on your bed, and be <u>still</u>."

The Quiet Regiment is a <u>challenging</u> one to implement because it takes <u>more</u> muscle power to keep the tongue <u>silent</u> than to move it.

James 1:19 reminds us that we are to be "<u>slow</u> to speak." Why? Because much of what we are <u>tempted</u> to say is not helpful.

Often it's <u>gossip</u>—a mixture of truth, partial truth, and outright untruth—that <u>hurts</u> everyone and <u>helps</u> no one. Even if it's the truth, you are under no <u>obligation</u> to transmit it.

Remember—if you say <u>nothing</u>, no one can <u>repeat</u> it! You can often be a great help to others by simply <u>listening</u>.

What others frequently need is a listening <u>ear</u>, not smart <u>comments</u> or empty <u>words</u>.

The Affirming Regimen

One of the most <u>famous</u> chapters of the entire Bible begins with these words: "If I speak with the tongues of men and of angels, but do not have love, I have become a <u>noisy</u> gong or a <u>clanging</u> cymbal" (1 Corinthians 13:1).

Cymbals have their place in an orchestra, but can you imagine the <u>insanity</u> they would cause if they were crashed <u>constantly</u> throughout an entire symphony?

Clanging gongs have their <u>place</u> in life—to wake us up, to warn us of fire, and alert us to danger.

However when they "stick," the sound becomes <u>deafening</u> and <u>irritating</u>." Jesus taught that there is <u>one</u> word that <u>summarizes</u> the entire Law: "You shall love the LORD your GOD with all your heart, and with all your soul, and with all your strength.' The second is this, 'You shall love your neighbor as yourself.' There is no other commandment greater than these" (Mark 12:30–31).

The WTIP who wants to <u>affirm</u> others is making great <u>progress</u> towards keeping God's holy Law. The greatest <u>obstacle</u> to grooming our tongues into affirming tongues is *gossip*.

It's one of the most <u>common</u> tongue diseases, is <u>highly</u> contagious, and is a sickness that leaves ugly <u>scars</u>.

Once the gossip <u>cycle</u> starts, it's almost <u>impossible</u> to stop it. We may be <u>sorry</u> about it, and we may be <u>forgiven</u> by God and the <u>slandered</u> person for it, but we can't undo the <u>consequences</u>.

Proverbs 17:9 teaches, "He who covers a transgression seeks love, but he who repeats a matter separates intimate friends." A good <u>rule</u> to follow is: if you wouldn't <u>say</u> it to a person's face, <u>don't</u> say it.

The Contented Regiment
Do you realize that the Israelites who escaped from the slave camps of Egypt were not <u>allowed</u> to enter the Promised Land?

Numbers 14:26–30 says it was because of their <u>complaining</u> tongues. A <u>grumbling</u>, complaining tongue is an <u>ugly</u> tongue, while a <u>contented</u> tongue is a beautiful tongue.

Philippians 2:14–15 teaches us that we are to "do all things without grumbling or disputing; that you may prove yourselves to be blameless and innocent, children of God in the midst of a crooked and perverse generation, among whom you appear as lights in the world."

Going through life with a complaining spirit is like <u>driving</u> a car with your eye constantly on the <u>rear</u>view mirror.

Instead of <u>complaining</u> about what you <u>don't</u> have, <u>practice</u> the <u>truth</u> of Philippians 3:13–14 and press forward to what lies ahead. In that way you will tone your tongue to be a contented tongue!

Concluding Comments

→ At the end of the age, we will be <u>judged</u> by how we have <u>used</u> our tongues.

→ Matthew 12:36 teaches that "for every idle word men may speak, they will give account of it in the day of judgment."

→ The tongue reveals <u>more</u> about us than almost anything else.

→ Although for a time the tongue may <u>hide</u> its true character, eventually it will be <u>discovered</u>.

→ Just as the mouth of a babbling spring reveals the <u>quality</u> of the water source, so our tongue <u>reveals</u> our heart (Matthew 12:35).

→ Before we prayed he asked one final question, "What type of Tongue <u>Grooming</u> Regimen will make your tongue a beautiful tongue?"

Bethany

Thank you, HF, for Pastor John's concern about our tongues. I know that mine needs all of the regiments he described tonight. I believe that You want me to begin with the Affirming Regiment. I know that I need to thank You for your many kindnesses to me first, then focus on others beginning with my parents.

? 4U

Beauty Consultation for My Tongue with the Interpretation

I compared my score on the Beauty Consultation for My Tongue with the Interpretation below and wrote a description of my results in my Quiet Time Journal.

- 41–37 a maturing, appreciative, quiet, affirming, contented tongue
- 36–33 a commitment to an appreciative, quiet, affirming, contented tongue
- 32–29 an understanding of what constitutes an appreciative, quiet, affirming, contented tongue
- 28–25 a minimal commitment to an appreciative, quiet, affirming, contented tongue
- 24–0 a tongue transplant is needed

I developed some goals that will assist me in cultivating an appreciative, quiet, affirming, and contented tongue.

I located some Scriptures that will assist me in training an appreciative, quiet, affirming, contented tongue. I also wrote out how the verse will help me. I started with Proverbs 15:1 I considered how the principle of prudent applies to this chapter.

I listed practical ways that I can apply the principle of prudent to my life. I am praying that my hF will motivate me to put the items on the list into action.

I studied the lives of two biblical examples of women who used their tongues in a positive and negative way and record examples of how Esther surrendered her will to God. was willing to take a risk and plead for her people, though she knew such boldness could cost her life.

I then took a look at Miriam and described how she along with her brother Aaron, criticized Moses and, thus, brought God's anger and judgment upon herself.

→ led the people astray.
→ forced the Israelites' progress toward the Promised Land to be halted for a week while she recovered from leprosy.

Finally, I evaluated how these examples affect the use of my tongue.

TLC

The end of the year is rapidly approaching, which means that our Health class is also drawing to a conclusion. Mrs. T. introduced the final topic for the year, Smart Home Management, to complement the information we have learned about smart eating, smart spending, and smart time management. She reminded us of the concepts we learned about functioning as a productive family member even if we have a job. It's important, according to Mrs. T., that we give our best efforts to our family rather than neglecting them for a job, sports, school assignments, or ministry. It's her desire that we learn to apply the information at home—thus her topic title, "Charity Begins at Home." We began with an interesting assignment

Instructions from Mrs. T.

→ Working with a partner and using your laptops find statistics that describe what family life is like in twenty-first-century America.
→ Be prepared to share your findings tomorrow.

Family Life in the Twenty-first Century
Family life today, according to the statistics, is not very good. One statistic reported that "The 'traditional' family (married couple with children under 18) has become much less prevalent in recent decades; the proportion of these families fell from 40 percent of all households in 1970 to 24 percent in 2000." Other statistics described abortion, the number of abortions in comparison to births each year, adoption, (which, from my perspective, is the right choice when compared to abortion), birth defects, births to unmarried women, domestic violence, illicit drug use by teens, marriage and divorce, remarriage, blended families, the number of women working outside of the home, the number of children living with birth parents, eating disorders among teens, and the number of obese Americans.

As our teams shared their statistics, the emotional tone in the classroom grew increasingly sober. Mrs. T. reminded us that we will establish the next generation of families. While these statistics are sobering, we can choose to learn skills that will make our homes happy, safe, and welcoming so that our families can contribute to positive rather than negative statistics. We are concluding our year in Family Living by studying home care. (I silently thanked my hF for being part of a happy traditional family.)

Quiet Time Notes from our Dinner Conversation Topic that focused on Helping to Make My Home a Welcoming Home

Gathering around the dinner table, Dad, Mom, and I shared the events of the day. The statistics about the decline of the family reported in my Family Living Class had made a strong impression on me, and I was grateful that Dad and Mom were willing to let me talk about my concerns. They listened carefully as I communicated my fears that if I marry I could one day be in the 76 percent of marriages that failed rather than the 24 percent statistical category of successful ones.

Dad gently reminded me that while there are no guarantees, even for Christians, that when a man and woman marry they will "live happily ever after." Both husband and wife have sin natures, and if they are not constantly choosing to follow the biblical teachings about marriage such as those found in Ephesians 5:22–33 small problems will grow into insurmountable ones.

Mom focused in on the reality that a marriage ceremony only changes the woman's name, not her character. If I want my home to home to fall into the 24 percent category, then I need to continually allow my hF to refine my character. She reminded me of the chart I prepared at the beginning of the school year when Mr. Solomon introduced the Six Pillars of Christian Character and taught us that character does count.

That study challenged me to cultivate a lifestyle that conforms me to the only Person who exhibited character in its purest form—Jesus Christ. She suggested that perhaps I need to turn my attention away from the fear that my marriage could fail to the truth that I need to allow my loving hF to conform me to His image. She also suggested that it's more important for me to become a young woman that pleases God rather than to look for "Mr. Right."

Separately, they hinted that it's the wife/mom's attitude that sets the tone for a welcoming home. Dad winked at Mom before stating, "If Mamma ain't happy, ain't nobody happy!" She tried to look offended but ended up laughing. Mom said that if I want my home to be a welcoming environment, I will practice now by making those who enter it feel welcome. That begins with submitting to my parents, joyfully completing my household tasks, and sincerely welcoming guests to our home.

We spent some time talking about the definition of the word welcome and concluded that it simply means that someone's arrival is joyfully anticipated. Mom believes that a wise woman, whether teen or senior citizen, first prepares her heart to welcome her family and guests and then prepares the home by making sure it's clean and comfortable.

We also talked about how important it is for those who live in the home to look forward to returning to it. If it's a place of order, those who live there will experience a sense of emotional well-being when they think of it. Mom said that is why she insists that my room is in good order before I leave for school. If I remember it as clean and peaceful, I will look forward to returning to it. If my mental image of it's one of disorder, then I will want to stay away as long as possible. Dad added that when he talks with people about returning to their homes they generally fall into two categories—those who can't wait to get there and those who can't wait to leave. He expressed gratitude to Mom for the welcoming environment that she has established for her family and the guests to whom we often extend hospitality.

Before we left the table, Dad suggested that we pray about our conversation. His gentle words calmed my fears and challenged my heart to focus on becoming a young woman who pleases God rather than meditating on the 76 percent marriage failure statistic.

As Mom and I cleaned up the kitchen, I asked her how she learned to be joyful in her practice of hospitality. She admitted that she used to dread to extend hospitality because she thought that her home and the food she prepared had to look like the glossy photos found in women's magazines. Then Dad challenged her to study the Scriptures and develop a biblical definition of hospitality. I decided to record her thoughts in my journal so that I can personally study the Scriptures she shared.

<u>Quiet Time Journal Notes—Joyfully Practicing Biblical Hospitality</u>

When hospitality is described in the Scriptures, there is an absence of instructions relating to the home décor, menu, or table setting. A journey through Scripture helps to paint a word portrait of biblical hospitality. John 14:15 and 21–24 clearly state that the primary evidence that individuals are Christians is their choice to obey their heavenly Father's commands. Though we live in a world that promotes "have things your own way," to please my heavenly Father I need to respond to all of His instructions with an obedient spirit, not just pick those that appeal to me—and that includes my response to what His Word teaches about hospitality.

I looked up the list of verses Mom has in the front of her hospitality notebook. This is what I learned.
- Romans 12:13b says that if I want to demonstrate obedience to my heavenly Father, I will practice hospitality.
- First Peter 4:9 reminds me that my attitude is very important. I am to practice hospitality without complaining. This verse

challenges me to examine my heart to discern whether I am approaching this opportunity to minister with a hearty attitude (Colossians 3:23 NASB).

- Hebrews 13:2 is a reminder that my willingness to offer hospitality may have far-reaching results. Abraham and Sarah (Genesis 18:1–3), Lot (Genesis 19:1–2), Gideon (Judges 6:11–24), and Manoah (Judges 13:6–20) all entertained strangers who were actually special messengers from God. While my motive should never be to give so that I will receive, Luke 6:38 states that the measuring cup I use to dispense my gifts and talents will be the same one used to provide my needs.
- Third John 7–8 challenges me to extend hospitality to those involved in ministry for our Lord. It's exciting to know that as I share my home and resources with the Lord's servants, I become an active part of their ministry.
- One of the requirements for individuals involved in church leadership, according to 1 Timothy 3:1–2 and Titus 1:7–8, is a willingness to allow others to visit them in their homes—the place where their character is most clearly seen.

Mom's Hospitality Strategies. Several days later, Mom and I enjoyed tea together as we discussed my findings. She complimented the depth of my understanding of the verses and then shared that the attitude of the apostle Paul is one that all women who desire to cultivate a heart of biblical hospitality will want to follow. She reflected on times when she tried to extend friendship to others and was met with rejection. She said that Satan tried to use the rejection as a roadblock to prevent her from obeying her heavenly Father on future occasions.

Dad helped her move beyond the roadblock by tenderly reminding her that about the life of the apostle Paul. He refused to dwell on the past or to drink of the cup of self-pity. Rather, he kept climbing higher toward his goal of Christlikeness all the days of his life. She learned that if she was going to cultivate a heart of biblical hospitality, she had to forget past grudges and rejection experiences, follow Paul's example, and

continue the ascent to the top of the "hospitality mountain."
She realized that to ascend to the top she needed proper
climbing strategies and that was when she started her hospitality notebooks. Having practiced hospitality for many years she
now has several notebooks. The strategies she used for her
first ones included:
- Collecting and filing simple, inexpensive recipes for desserts
  and meals.
- Making a list of people who would be encouraged by her
  offer of hospitality.
- Starting simple. She began by spontaneously inviting people
  home after church.
- Praying that her loving heavenly Father would give her joy
  in practicing hospitality to others.

Remembering that memories require time and energy to create.
Choosing to nurture a heart for biblical hospitality that sincerely communicates, "Come back soon."

Since I will soon be going to college and will have more
opportunities to extend hospitality, she suggested that I
begin my own hospitality notebook. She showed me her list of
HOSPITALITUDES. Since it was a word I had not heard before
she told me that she created it to help her have the right
attitude about practicing biblical hospitality. It comes from the
word hospitality, meaning "to pursue the love of strangers"
(Romans 12:13; Hebrews 13:2) and beatitude, meaning the character of true faith. She encouraged me to word process the
HOSPITALITUDES that are most meaningful to me and place them
at the front of my notebook. From her office supplies we
selected a new notebook, sheet protectors, and pretty paper.
Once I finished my homework this evening I spent some time
prayerfully considering the hospitalitudes and selected these to
begin my notebook.

Hospitalitudes

Happy are those…

who practice biblical hospitality, because in so doing they are demonstrating their love for God (1 John 3:17–18).

who "pursue the love of strangers," for they are obeying their heavenly Father's command and modeling His character (Romans 12:13b NASB).

in church leadership who practice hospitality, for they allow others to observe them in their homes, where their character is most graphically revealed (1 Timothy 3:1–2; Titus 1:5–8).

who include people of all cultures on their guests lists, for in this manner they are demonstrating the expansive love of their heavenly Father (John 3:16).

who are willing to make the sacrifice to practice hospitality, for they understand the importance of creating memories (Exodus 12:1–14).

who develop hospitality management skills, for in this way they are being faithful stewards of all that our Lord has provided for them (1 Corinthians 4:2).

whose homes are both a place of refuge and a center for evangelism, for they are glorifying their heavenly Father by their actions (1 Peter 2:11–12) and fulfilling His instructions "to do the work of an evangelist" (2 Timothy 4:5).

who have consecrated their lives to their heavenly Father, for they are capable of practicing true biblical hospitality (2 Corinthians 4:7).

who don't become disillusioned in practicing biblical hospitality, for they understand that in due time they will reap if they don't grow weary (Galatians 6:9).

who acknowledge that they are unable to practice biblical hospitality in their own strength, for they know that our Lord's power overcomes their weaknesses and allows them to become vessels for His honor and glory (2 Corinthians 12:9–10; Philippians 4:13).

Dear HF, thank You for the listening ears and godly advice of my parents about the statistics that troubled me. I pray that You will help me focus on becoming a young woman who pleases You rather than always looking for "Mr. Right." Thanks too about what I learned about practicing biblical hospitality. Please help me apply what Your Word says about hospitality so that the hospitalitudes will be evident in my life.

Family Studies Lecture Handout: Practical Home Care
The opening PowerPoint slide of Mrs. T's lesson on home care was one of chaos and disorder. Of course, when someone said that it looked like their room—we all laughed, but inwardly I hoped that was not true. Moving on, she shared that for a home to run smoothly it needs to be cared for daily.

Creating a Smart Home Care Plan
The words <u>clean</u> and <u>neat</u> have different definitions for each family. The most <u>important</u> point is for <u>everyone</u> in the family to feel that it's a place where they are <u>protected</u>, can stay <u>healthy</u>, and are <u>comfortable</u> in extending *hospitality* to others. A <u>home</u> *care* <u>plan</u> is necessary for home to be a nurturing place for family members.

Smart home care means <u>planning</u> how <u>best</u> to use your family's energy, time, money, and skill.
• It means choosing <u>cleaning</u> techniques that get the tasks done as completely as possible.
• It also means that <u>everyone</u> in the family helps so that no one person (like Mom) has too much to do and so everyone has a <u>vested</u> interest in keeping the home maintained once it's cleaned. The motto, "<u>many</u> hands make <u>light</u> work" is true in the upkeep of a home.

How much *home care* needs to be done depends on:
• The <u>size</u> of the family.
• The <u>ages</u> of family members.
• <u>Indoor</u> hobbies and activities.
• Hospitality <u>styles</u>.
• The size and age of the <u>home</u>.
• The <u>types</u> of furnishings.
• The <u>presence</u> of pets.
• Geographically where the home is <u>located</u>. <u>We in the high desert need to dust often.</u>
• The <u>weather</u> and season.

A *smart home care plan* includes these <u>steps</u>:
• <u>Analyze</u> your needs and set <u>cleaning</u> *goals* (remember IDK?).

- Take the _time_ to look over _each_ room.
- Identify _clutter_, cobwebs, dirt, or dust.
- In hard-to see _areas_ do the _touch test_ by running a _clean_ finger over furnishings and surfaces to find _dirt_ that may not be easily seen.

1. _Ask_ yourself, "What _jobs_ need to be done?" and then _list_ them.
2. Set _priorities_. _Rank_ the _home–care tasks_ from _most_ to _least_ important.
3. _Number_ the _cleaning tasks_ in the order in which they _need_ to be done.
4. Develop a _smart home care plan_ for each _room_ and each _task_. A part of preparing the plan is to answer some important _questions_:

- How _often_ does the room or specific task _need_ to be done?
    When will it be done?
    Who will do it?
    How much _time_ will it take?
    What _supplies_, tool, or other materials are _needed_ to do it?
- Make a _schedule_. Assign the _cleaning tasks_ to certain days of the _week_. With a schedule, the family can _plan_ the workload to use everyone's _abilities_, personal schedules, and _time_. A schedule lets family members _know_ when their tasks need to be _completed_. It _divides_ the _cleaning tasks_ according to age, ability level, and time schedules.
- Allow for _flexibility_. A _flexible schedule_ allows for job _trading_ and _changing_ the days on which certain jobs are done to meet family member's _special_ needs. Remember to _custom-design_ your schedule to meet your family's needs. Another family's schedule might serve as a model for yours, but it's unlikely that it would be exactly the same.
- Consider _rotating_ the tasks periodically. This allows _everyone_ to experience all of the _cleaning tasks_ so all have an _appreciation_ of what it takes to do the task.
- Use the _room-by-room_ method of _cleaning_ whenever possible. This _method_ is usually more effective than completing random tasks.

- Include larger <u>seasonal</u> *cleaning tasks* in the schedule. Washing the windows, cleaning the garage, stripping and waxing the floors, and cleaning under the refrigerator are not done weekly but need to be <u>included</u> in the schedule to insure the entire home is <u>well-maintained</u>.
- <u>Evaluate</u> your *Home Care Schedule* to make sure you are <u>working smart</u>. It's important that the *plan* <u>simplifies</u> your *cleaning tasks*. Some evaluation questions might include:
- Does the *schedule* include <u>daily</u> tasks such as pick-up clutter, making the beds, and hanging up clothes or putting them in the hamper?
- Does the *schedule* encourage a <u>room-by-room</u> cleaning so that each room gets the special care it needs?
- Do I save <u>energy</u> by having cleaning tools and supplies collected <u>before</u> I begin cleaning?
- Do I <u>alternate</u> difficult tasks and easy tasks?
- Do I take a brief <u>rest</u> after a difficult cleaning task or in the <u>middle</u> of a long work period?
- During the brief rest do I <u>increase</u> my energy with a healthy <u>snack</u>? A cold glass of juice can help the mind and muscles feel <u>refreshed</u>.
- Do I refresh my mind with <u>soothing</u> music?
- Does the *schedule* include <u>rotating</u> *cleaning tasks* so that they don't become <u>boring</u>?
- Does the *schedule* contain <u>larger</u> seasonal *cleaning tasks*?
- Are you <u>constantly</u> looking for ways to work *smarter* rather than harder?

Mrs. T's final slide displayed the same room as the first slide with one major difference—it reflected that a *smart home care* had been applied to it.

→ <u>Note homework assignment.</u>

?4U

- I conducted an Internet search and created my own set of statistics that describes what family life is like in twenty-first-century America.
- I used the Ideal Man worksheet in the WTIP section of my notebook to research some of the character qualities that should be evident in a guy I would consider dating.
- Once I have developed it I considered my own character. I identified what needs to be changed in my own life so that I can focus on becoming a young woman who pleases God rather than finding "Mr. Right."
- I prayerfully committed the character changes to my hF. I asked Bethany to hold me accountable for growth in each of the areas where character changes are needed.
- I began a hospitality notebook. I started with Mom's suggestions and then added my own creativity.
- I used Mrs. Titus' project example to prepare a smart home care plan for my room, implemented it for two weeks, and then evaluated it. I then made the modifications necessary to insure that I am working smarter rather than harder.
- Once I master the smart home care plan for my room I will work with my Mom to develop a Smart Home Care plan for our entire home. I will make sure it includes all family members.
- I listed the ways that the principle of loveable applies to this topic.
- I wrote in my Quite Time Journal practical ways that I can apply the principle of loveable to my life. I am praying that my hF will motivate me to put my thoughts into action.
- I studied the life of Hannah (1 Samuel 1:9–28) and
- Described the tasks she performed that proved she was loveable.
- Wrote in my Quiet Time Journal how the tasks she completed affected her future.
- I also studied the life of Peninnah and
- Described the tasks she performed that proved she was not loveable.
- Wrote in my Quiet Time Journal how her actions affected her future.

Break

Mom poked her head in the family room as Bethany and I were finishing preparation for this week's small group meeting. We are planning a special surprise for the younger women in the group to reinforce the Titus Two Principle we studied right before the holidays. "When you ladies are finished, I would like to chat with you for a few minutes. Please come and get me when you are done." We wrapped up the final details, prayed, and then summoned Mom. She returned carrying a tray with three mugs of hot chocolate and some of her yummy cookies. We were ready for the snack.

Sitting in her favorite chair, she stirred her chocolate and then asked if we might consider accompanying her to the women's conference that was to be held at the Anaheim Convention Center in several weeks. I knew the convention center was across the street from Disneyland but was unaware of the conference. Bethany's eyes widened, however, as Mom spoke. "Mrs. Abramson," Bethany began, "do you mean the Titus Two Woman Conference?" Mom nodded an affirmative answer. "Posters and brochures are all over the college campus, but even the student rate is pretty pricey. Are you sure you want me to go?" "Yes," Mom quickly stated. "You continue to be a great source of joy and encouragement to Sarah and I thought it would be a small way I could thank you. As well, I will have a book table at the event, and I thought perhaps you ladies could help to manage it." Bethany and I made eye contact, put our thumbs up, and in unison said, "Yes!" "Wonderful," Mom responded, "I will make our reservations for the Disneyland hotel tomorrow."

Several Fridays later Mom picked me up at school and Bethany at the college. We headed south to Anaheim and arrived in plenty of time to set up the book table, enjoy our dinner at the hotel, and dress for the evening. Mom always looks great but I noticed that she seemed to be giving extra special attention to her grooming this evening. As we took the hotel shuttle to the convention center, Bethany and I could hardly sit still.

As soon as we arrived, Mom got Bethany and me established at the book table and disappeared. Shortly before the opening session she summoned us to the filled-to-capacity convention hall. We were surprised that she had seats for us in the front row.

The conference was opened in prayer by the president of the Titus Two ministry and then we enjoyed a time of worship by a well-known artist. As the hostess approached the microphone to introduce the speaker for the evening, I recognized her because I had seen her picture on the front of one of Mom's women's ministry magazines. She began her introductory remarks that I've saved here.

My eyes filled with tears as Mom gracefully and confidently stepped to the podium.

Titus Two Program

"As you know, it is the policy of the Titus Two ministry to not publicize the speakers for our annual conference. We do this because we want our attendees to come because God wants them here rather than coming simply because they are impressed by the speakers. It has been a number of years since I have had the privilege of introducing our keynote speaker for this year's conference. She was a part of this conference 18 years ago, though not the key-note speaker. Her first book had recently been released and we were excited to have her share her passion for God's special instructions to women to our conference attendees. However, as the date approached she was concerned that she was not going to be able to fulfill her commitment because of her recurring flu-like symptoms. Much prayer was lifted on her behalf and God miraculously strengthened her and allowed her to participate.

As she stood before us she told us that she would not be speaking at conferences for some time because God had graciously opened her womb, and she was expecting the child that doctors told her she would never have. We chose her as this year's keynote speaker because throughout the past 18 years her message to women has increased in credibility as she chose to daily live out the Titus 2:3-5 Principle in her home. Please join me in welcoming Liz Abramson as this year's Titus Two Woman keynote speaker!"

"Thank you for that warm introduction. It's a special privilege to be a part of this year's conference. As we begin our session, I would like to introduce you to the precious young woman I was carrying 18 years ago, Sarah Joy. I have treasured every day of her life and would not trade the joy of being her mother for anything. She will be graduating from high school next month and begins her college education in the fall. For that reason I now have a bit more time to be a part of events like this one.

"I would also like for you to meet her small-group leader, Bethany, who has modeled a *servant's heart* for Sarah. She was most influential in Sarah's choice to attend The Master's College where she will major in Home Economics-Family and Consumer Sciences—a major designed to train its students to become women who please God. This session is dedicated to both of them because it is my prayer for them and for each attendee this evening that they and you will always choose to enthusiastically embrace God's special instructions to women." Bethany and I simply stared at one another. Though I knew that the words Mom was going to speak were for everyone in the convention center, as I listened to them it was as if we were sitting in the family room chatting together.

Choosing to Become a Titus Two Woman
If we are going to be known as Titus Two Women we will make *cultivating* a lifestyle that pleases our hF our top *priority*.

Choosing such a lifestyle means that we must *think* like Him, and to think like Him we must have His *mind*.

Proverbs 1:7 explains *how* to know our heavenly Father's mind…we reverence Him. "This reverential awe and admiring, submissive fear is foundational for all spiritual knowledge and wisdom. The fear of the Lord is a state of mind in which one's own attitudes, will, feelings, deeds and goals are exchanged for God's." *Failure* to exchange our attitudes, will, feelings, deeds, and goals for God's will makes us *vulnerable* to assimilating the *fraudulent* standards of man's wisdom.

The voices of twenty-first-century society shout loudly to us to free or liberate ourselves from the *bondage* of our ancestors, "do our own thing," *demand* equality, gain personal fulfillment in life regardless of the impact on others, take control of our bodies, and many other *contradictions* to God's special instructions to women bombard us. Scripture is clear that God's general *purpose* for all believers is to be *conformed* to the *image* of Christ (Romans 8:29), bear *fruit* (John 15:1–11), walk in the Spirit (Galatians 5:16–26), exhibit *conduct* that reflects their salvation (Ephesians 4:1–3), be good stewards of all of their *resources* (1 Timothy 6:17–19), and eagerly *anticipate* His return (2 Timothy 4:8).

As Titus Two Women we will not only *choose* a lifestyle that reflects God's general purpose, we will search the Scriptures *eagerly* to discover His special *instructions* to us.

This reality is true for all of the Scriptures that provide instructions for choosing a lifestyle that allows us to be 'doers of the word, and not merely hearers who delude themselves' (James 1:22).

When we search the Scriptures we find that a Titus Two Woman is…
- Aware that she was made by God in His own image (Genesis 1:27).
- Gracious (Proverbs 11:16).
- Tactful (Proverbs 11:22).
- Careful to build her house following the way of wisdom described in Proverbs 9:1–6 and Proverbs 14:1.
- Worthy of praise (Ruth 3:11, Proverbs 31:10–31).
- Cautious to avoid cultivating the behaviors associated with a seductress (Ecclesiastes 7:26–28).
- Guarded in her behavior to prevent acquiring a reputation like the daughters of Zion (Isaiah 3:16–24).
- Modest, her clothing reflecting that her heart is focused on God—especially for worship (1 Timothy 2:9).
- Trustworthy in all aspects of her life and ministry (1 Timothy 3:11).
- Grounded in the Word of God (2 Timothy 3:6–7).
- Careful to develop a personal testimony that is consistent with her profession of faith (1 Timothy 2:10).
- Teachable (1 Timothy 2:11).
- Available to teach the younger women (Titus 2:3–5).
- Excited about developing the type of character that pleases her heavenly Father (1 Peter 3:1–6—see chapter 10).
- Faithful to follow the examples of the women who walk through the pages of the Old and New Testament (1 Corinthians 10:6; Hebrews 11:11; 1 Peter 3:1–6).

(Mom then shared a bit of her personal testimony. I have heard it before but tonight these thoughts made a very strong impression on me.)

"A Bit About Liz Abramson:

"Though I grew up in a Christian home and thought I accepted Christ at the age of ten at Vacation Bible School, I didn't mature as a believer. As I entered my teen years and my elderly parents' health declined, I acquired a negative, cynical outlook on life. My father passed away during the first week of my freshman year of college; and my mother, my second day as a new teacher. I recall my pastor putting his arm around me at my mother's funeral and saying, 'We'll see you in church on Sunday.' Outwardly, I simply nodded my head. Inwardly I thought, 'I have attended church since I was an infant. It has done nothing for me, and I have better things to do with my Sundays.' As I settled into my role as a new professional, from outward appearances my life appeared ideal—I had a good job, a boyfriend, and discretionary financial resources for the first time in my life, a compatible roommate, and was in an upward career track in my profession.

"Despite all of the 'good things' that were happening externally, I experienced an internal, gnawing hunger. I vividly recall returning home from a date one Friday night and saying to my roommate, 'I don't know what you are doing Sunday, but I am going to church.' Since she didn't have other plans she agreed to attend with me. I didn't want to return to my childhood church so we attended one about a mile from home. Tim LaHaye was the pastor, and before we left the church that Sunday, individually, we both made certain that we were a part of God's family (see Romans 3:10, 3:23, 5:8, 5:12, 6:23, 10:9–11, 10:13, 1 Corinthians 5:17).

"As an educated woman, I was excited to learn both from a gifted pastor and study the Word of God on my own (Pastor LaHaye consistently repeated, 'No Bible, no breakfast!'). I experienced an insatiable hunger for spiritual truth—and as the weeks passed, I experienced a decline in my internal, gnawing hunger. The glamour subsided, however, when I was confronted with biblical standards about the role of women. As with Eve of old, Satan tried his lie on me—'surely your *loving* heavenly Father did not mean that you, an educated woman, would be subjected to those archaic standards!' (Genesis 3:1–7). By God's grace I didn't linger to discuss the matter with him but rather continued 'to grow in the grace and knowledge of our Lord and Savior Jesus Christ' (2 Peter 3:18). As a result of my growth I have learned that...

My heavenly Father does not offer a "cafeteria plan" for obedience (James 2:8–13). We live in a world that promotes, 'Have things your own way.' I learned that to please my heavenly Father I needed to respond to *all* of His instructions with an obedient spirit (2 Samuel 15:22; Psalm 51:16–17) not just pick those that appealed to me. I also learned that asking forgiveness rather than permission was an unacceptable behavior (James 4:17).

God's Word is true whether or not I choose to embrace its teaching (Hebrews 4:12–13). I began to mature spiritually at a time when mini-skirts were the rage—and though my skirts were not *as* short as some others, they were definitely shorter than what belonged on a woman desiring to reflect godly character. It seemed that every time my friend and I attended a worship service Pastor LaHaye somehow integrated skirt lengths into the sermon (his recurring statement went something like, 'Children used to hide behind their mother's skirts—now they can't reach them!'). "Roast pastor" was often one of the entrees for our Sunday lunch, and we frequently questioned one another with, 'What is *his* problem?' Again, however, as we <u>studied</u> the Scriptures and desired to <u>respond in</u> obedience to them, we found that we chose to lengthen our skirts (1 Timothy 2:9; 1 Peter 3:1–6). It was not long until we realized that the problem was not Pastor LaHaye's, but ours.

My Creator has no obligation to explain His reasoning to me (Isaiah 45:9, Romans 11:33–36). I learned a valuable lesson from my parents that helped immensely in my spiritual growth. As a child, I often lacked the maturity to understand the reasons that motivated their decisions. However, as I matured, I gradually began to understand why they insisted that I follow their instructions or why their answer was sometimes "no" to my heartfelt pleas. My father often said that as I increased in age, he gained more wisdom."

(Dad says this about me too—and he seldom changed his reasoning.) What had changed is that my relationship to my father had matured, and he had proved credible over a long period of time. The same thing is true in our relationship with our heavenly Father. At times we make a judgment about the validity of His instructions before we have cultivated a trustworthy relationship with Him. Second Peter 3:18 is a great motivating verse for all women who desire to practice the Titus Two Principle. The more we grow in the knowledge of Christ, the more His character will be reflected in our lives and the less concerned we will be about understanding all of the "whys."

I must exercise faith to embrace teaching that is contrary to cultural trends (Hebrews 11:6). I am to trust my heavenly Father that there is "no good thing that He would withhold from me if I was walking uprightly" (Psalm 84:11) when His instructions deviate from what society says will make me happy. My only responsibility is to make sure that I am choosing to walk uprightly—and that is an act of the will, not the emotions."[12]

A hush settled over the convention center as Mom brought her message to a conclusion. She closed in prayer, and then asked if there were questions. I wrote on my handout some of the ones that were most applicable to me.:

(These are some of the questions people asked Mom.)

Question and Answer Session

Is it really possible to choose a lifestyle that pleases God in the twenty-first century? Absolutely!

The only way others know that we belong to our hF is by our lifestyle. Scripture teaches us that our lives are to reflect our heavenly Father's character so that others are drawn to Him (Matthew 5:14–16). I know, however, that I can't live such a lifestyle in my own strength. I also know that Philippians 4:13 says that I can do *all* things by relying on Christ's strength.

Why is a godly lifestyle so important—after all, we do live in the twenty-first century?
A godly life gives convincing testimony of the saving power of God that brings HIM glory (1 Peter 2:11–12).

How do you try to show Christ by how you live?
I attempt to show Christ by:
- Hiding God's Word in my heart so that I won't sin against Him (Psalm 119:11).
- Choosing to be *content* rather than complaining about my circumstances. Paul teaches us that contentment is an acquired character quality, not a natural response (Philippians 4:11; 1 Timothy 6:6).
- Desiring to "walk in the Spirit and not fulfill the lust of the flesh" (Galatians 5:16).
- Exercising faith to embrace biblical teaching that is contrary to cultural trends (Hebrews 11:6).
- Believing that there is no GOOD thing that He will withhold from me if I choose to live by His standards (Psalm 84:11).

How does a twenty-first-century Christian woman develop self-control?
Self-control, as are the other eight qualities listed in Galatians 5:22–23, is an indication that one has a personal relationship with Jesus Christ. Galatians 5:16 tells us that "walking in the Spirit" is a command, not an option. Walking in the Spirit is a continuous action rather than occasional obedience. As we mature as believers, walking in the Spirit becomes increasingly more of an automatic reflex rather than a battle between the spirit and the flesh (Galatians 5:17–21). When a person continues to walk in the flesh there is a good possibility that they don't have a personal relationship with Jesus Christ. Self-control is not a natural human response. We grow in the character quality of self-control by believing that we don't have to be a victim to Satan's lie that we can't be different than our natural instincts.

How do you continue to grow in the area of self-control?
I continue to grow in the area of self-control by:
- Acknowledging that a reaction that does not reflect self-control is sin and asking my heavenly Father to forgive me (1 John 1:9).
- Pursuing reconciliation by humbly seeking forgiveness from those I have offended without blaming them for my wrong response (Matthew 5:23–24). Phrasing such as, "I was wrong when I *(fill in the offense)*. Will you forgive me?" allows me to accept personal responsibility without casting blame on the offended person.

- Asking someone to hold me accountable for my desire to exhibit self-control (James 5:16). This someone in my husband who sees my response to a variety of situations.
- Choosing to think on those things that promote self-control (Philippians 4:8–9).
- Consistently thanking my hF for the progress I am making (1 Thessalonians 5:18).
- Believing that I can be a victor rather than a victim in maturing in this character quality (Philippians 4:13).
- Being patient with my progress (Philippians 1:6).
- Journaling my successes (Psalm 103).

Is it possible to develop a gentle and quiet spirit when society screams at us to be the opposite of these character qualities?
Cultivating a *gentle and quiet spirit* is incredibly important for a Titus Two Woman. 1 Peter 3:3–6 reminds us that having a gentle and quiet or humble spirit is precious in the sight of our heavenly Father (that is why I chose *Precious in His Sight* as the title for one of my books). However, gentle does not mean that I am like a rag doll that flops about. Rather, I am to exhibit strength under the control of the Holy Spirit (Galatians 5:22–23).

How do you continue to develop a gentle and quiet spirit?
I continue to grow in the area of a *gentle and quiet spirit* by:
- Acknowledging that the absence of gentleness in my life reflects a prideful attitude—the first thing that my hF HATES! (Proverbs 6:16–19).
- Accepting that developing a *gentle and quiet spirit* is one of the ways that I show my respect and love for my heavenly Father (1 Peter 3:3).
- Realizing that a submissive response to circumstances that I don't like is a way that I practice having a *gentle and quiet spirit* (Colossians 3:12). My Lord set the example for me by accepting punishment He didn't deserve without seeking revenge (1 Peter 2:18–25).
- Having a teachable spirit (James 1:21).
- Being considerate of others—even when they provoke me (Ephesians 4:2).

- Asking someone to hold me accountable for my desire to exhibit a gentle and quiet spirit (James 5:16). Again, this is someone in my home setting who sees my response to a variety of situations. Usually it is my husband, but sometimes it is Sarah Joy.
- Choosing to think on those things that promote gentleness (Philippians 4:8–9).
- Consistently thanking my heavenly Father for the progress I am making (1 Thessalonians 5:18).

As with the quality of *self-control,* I must believe that I can be a victor rather than a victim in maturing in this character quality (Philippians 4:13). I must be patient with my progress (Philippians 1:6), and journaling my successes (Psalm 103) helps me to focus on how far I have come rather than how far I still have to go.

Titus Two Women in progress we MUST keep moving forward, following the role model of the Apostle Paul (Philippians 3:12–16). Though this is not a popular concept in today's Christian culture, if we choose to cultivate an appetite for the character qualities described in Galatians 5:22–23 we will "walk in the Spirit and not fulfill the lust of the flesh" (Galatians 5:16).

What situations do you see in the world today that challenge Christians to maintain a godly lifestyle?
2 Timothy 3:1–17 describes the twenty-first century culture clearly. It also provides Christians with the formula to live as Christians in these difficult times even when those who profess to be Christians lead lifestyles and have appetites that are contrary to the Scriptures. I encourage you to make a list of descriptions of "the last days" described in this passage and then examine current news for examples of the events outlined in 2 Timothy 3:1–17. At the conclusion of your study I think you will see why Scripture commands us to "be careful how we walk" (Ephesians 5:15–21).

As the hostess indicated that it was time to conclude the session, Mom closed in prayer asking that our gracious heavenly Father would apply her teaching to each attendee in the convention center and that they would always choose to be Titus Two Women regardless of how the culture tempts them to do otherwise!

Thank You, HF, for my mom. She never resented putting aside her professional speaking to fulfill God's special instructions to wives and moms. I know from my friends that this is rare today. The Convention Hostess is right; Mom's choice 18 years ago increased her credibility as she presented Your special instructions to women tonight. Thank You for the privilege of being her daughter. I pray that I will always follow her example and choose to be a Titus Two Woman. In Your name I pray, amen.

?4U

- I listed the ways the principle of God-fearing apply to this topic.
- I wrote in my Quiet Time Journal practical ways that I can apply the principle of God-fearing to my life. I am praying that my hF will motivate me to put the items on the list into action.
- I spent a month (I selected one with 31 days) studying the Book of Proverbs.
- I looked for and record examples of both the Wise and Foolish Woman.
- I described how my behavior aligns with theirs.
- I set personal goals that will help me focus on my behavior on becoming a Wise Teen.
- I shared the goals with Bethany who will hold me accountable for integrating them into my life.
- I used the Scriptures presented in this chapter, and supported them with my own Scripture search, to formulate a Life Mission Statement that reflects my understanding of God's Special Instructions to Women.
- I studied the life of Anna (Luke 2:22-27, 36-38) and
- I Described the tasks she performed that proved she was God-fearing.
- I Reported how the tasks she completed affected her future.
- I also studied the life of Eve (Genesis 1:27-28, 2:18, 20-25, 3:1-20) and
- I Described her actions that suggest she was not God-fearing.
- I Reported how her actions affected her future as well as the future of others.

The End and Begin

Just as Pastor John planned a special event in August for the members of the high school group who are graduating this year, he planned a second for the Sunday afternoon before graduation.

He began our time together by asking the question:

"How many of you experienced a no regret senior year?" Almost in unison thumbs went up around the room. By God's grace and great accountability from one another, our leaders, as well as Pastor John, we could say that we:

- Gave up our personal RIGHTS (1 Corinthians 13:4–8).
- Lived so there would be no REGRETS (Philippians 3:13–14; Hebrews 12:1–2; 2 Timothy 4:7–8).
- REJOICED instead of complaining (Philippians 4:4–8).
- Anticipated the REWARD (Hebrews 10:35–39).
- He then began his topic for the event, "Pressing Forward" based on Philippians 3:12–14.

168—Pressing Forward

The Apostle Paul presents four keys to the worthy walk in Philippians 3:12–14 that provides direction to the twenty-first-century WTIP:

- a genuine restlessness (Philippians 3:12)
- a solitary longing (Philippians 3:13).
- a wholehearted purpose (Philippians 3:12, 14), and
- a definite goal (Philippians 3:13, 14). Paul's genuine restlessness is a model for all believers.

⇨ While he was satisfied with his Savior and his salvation, he was dissatisfied with his flesh.

⇨ He was restless with his spiritual status because he was not all that he knew that he could or should be.

⇨ Paul uses the analogy of a runner to describe the Christian's spiritual growth.

⇨ The believer has not reached his goal of Christlikeness, but like the runner in a race, he must continue to pursue it.

⇨ The Christian life is to be exciting, and as WTIPs, we should be excited about growing, regardless of our spiritual age.

⇨ Paul's solitary longing helps us to eliminate the unnecessary from our lives.

⇨ Our quest toward Christlikeness puts life into a single focus!

Paul says, "This one thing I do."

⇨ As WTIPs we are to have only one goal—to serve God with our entire being (1 Corinthians 6:12).

⇨ Our Lord Jesus serves as the ultimate role model for this solitary longing. He didn't finish all the urgent tasks in Palestine or all the things He would have liked to do, but He did finish the work God gave Him to do.

⇨ Paul's wholehearted purpose helped him to focus on his determination to keep moving toward the goal.

⇨ We will not succeed if we don't have a strong determination. However, the source of our strength must be the Holy Spirit, not simply our determination (Philippians 4:13).

A sobering question—as WTIPs, "are we mature enough to keep pursuing our "upward call" (Philippians 3:14) when it would be easier to quit? Finally, Paul had a definite goal, and he moved toward it with determination. (I need to pray about this question!)

Serving God with our entire being challenges us to refuse to dwell on the past—regardless of whether it is filled with success or sin.
What we are today is what counts!

Paul challenges us to refuse to drink from the cup of self-pity and to release past grudges and incidents of mistreatment. He forgot these and climbed higher toward his goal!"

"As I conclude my final message to you, I want to focus on the change that will occur in our relationship. "I move from your High School Pastor to the role of mentor with the goals of challenging you to...

• Apply the truths learned and fulfill the commitments made throughout your time in the high school group. Become dissatisfied with the gap between confessional and functional theology.

• Stimulate the application of James 1:22.

• Cultivate a desire to model our Lord's servant's heart (Matthew 20:20–28)."

"Often, the pursuit of these goals begins with an act of the will—that is doing the right thing and then allowing our emotions to catch up with the action."

You will recall we often discussed that the entire Book of Psalms is directed to our will, not our emotions.

As a group we have spent much time integrating biblical role models into our study of God's Word.

Before we celebrate with the wonderful dinner that was prepared in your honor, you are going to divide into small groups of guys and girls.

I am going to give each group a list of men and women who are recorded in the Scriptures.

Using the statement, "I will," you are to develop statements that challenge you to keep "Pressing Forward." Here is an example to get you started. Like Paul, I will forget those things that are behind and press forward."

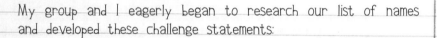

My group and I eagerly began to research our list of names and developed these challenge statements:

I WILL, LIKE...

- The Queen of Sheba, diligently seek godly wisdom (1 Kings 10:1-13);
- Ruth, respond to the advice of older women (Ruth 3:11);
- Sarah, submit to those in authority over me (1 Peter 3:6);
- The little Jewish Maid, boldly, but appropriately, speak of my faith (1 Kings 5:1-14);
- Esther, choose to take risks to further God's kingdom (Esther 4:1-17);
- The Widow of Zarephath, trust my heavenly Father to multiply my resources (1 Kings 17:10-24);
- The Shunammite Woman, extend hospitality (2 Kings 4:8-37);
- Mary, the Mother of Jesus, wholeheartedly declare myself a bondslave of the Lord (Luke 1:26-38);
- Elizabeth, believe that God works miracles in women of all ages (Luke 1:5-25);
- Mary of Bethany, listen with a teachable spirit, to My Master's Words (Luke 10:38-41);

- The poor widow, give out of my need rather than my abundance (Mark 12:42);
- Mary, exhibit humble love and devotion for my Lord (John 12:2–3);
- The woman with the lost coin, approach each responsibility with determination (Luke 15:8–10);
- Dorcas, share my talents with those in need (Acts 9:36–43);
- Lydia, choose to use my profession for my Lord's glory (Acts 16:14, 40);
- Lois and Eunice, try to leave a godly heritage (2 Timothy 1:5);
- The Wise Woman of Proverbs, purpose to fear my Lord (Proverbs 31:10–31).

Realizing that I can't hope to achieve these goals in my own strength—I will rely upon my Lord...for I can do all things through Christ who strengthens me (Philippians 4:13).

As we finished our statements, prayer was offered for the scrumptious meal that awaited us. Dinner conversation centered on the challenge statements each group developed. It was the end of our high school years together and the beginning of new opportunities to press forward!

Today was the final all-school assembly at West Ranch High. It seems, in many ways, that Mr. Solomon had just introduced the theme for the school year—It's What's Inside That Counts. As he made his introductory remarks, he reminded us that it was his hope that during this school year we would be more concerned about our character (who we are inside) than how we looked or what we have. This time rather than beginning his presentation with the question, "Character—What Is It?" he asked, "What freshman, sophomore, junior, and senior best exemplified the Six Pillars of Character throughout the year?" Throughout the auditorium, names were suggested. He reminded us that he had announced at that first assembly that at the conclusion of the school year an award would be presented to a freshman, sophomore, junior, and senior who had best exemplified the Six Pillars of Character throughout the year. Now was the time to announcement the award recipients.

Beginning the PowerPoint presentation, he refreshed our memory on the award selection procedures. Students were first nominated by their peers (I remembered filling out the forms) and then approved by the faculty and staff to avoid the awards simply being a popularity contest. Before announcing the award recipients, he affirmed the entire student body for a terrific year because most of the students chose to exemplify

Trustworthiness	Fairness
Respect	Caring
Responsibility	Citizenship

He then announced the freshman, sophomore, and junior awards. Much applause followed the awarding of each. The description of the senior recipient was introduced with the statement, "I would like to share with you what this person's peers, teachers, and the staff wrote about her:

- She is someone to look up to.
- I have never seen her take something that belongs to some-one else.
- Does what she says she will do even when it is inconvenient.
- Does not show partiality.
- Is gracious.
- Speaks encouraging words.
- Does what she is supposed to do with a good attitude!
- West Ranch High School is a better school because she is one of its students.

"PLEASE JOIN ME IN CONGRATULATING SARAH JOY ABRAMSON!"

I was stunned. . . . My friends pushed me out of my chair, and I somehow managed to walk down the aisle and up the stairs to be stage. Mr. Solomon shook my hand, handed me a beautiful plaque with the Six Pillars of Character engraved on it and an envelope. He then stated that the envelope contained a letter confirming that all of my expenses for the first year of col-lege were paid for by an anonymous benefactor and that the scholarship is renewable for up to four years. As I descended the stairs I saw Dad. Mom, and Bethany standing in the back of the auditorium. Dad held a bouquet of my favorite flowers, pink roses, Mom a cluster of balloons, and Bethany a sign that simply stated, "REWARDED, PROVERBS 31:31." All three of them wiped away tears. So did I!

The remainder of the assembly was a blur to me. In the midst of all of the excitement I just had to bow my head and thank my heavenly Father for the "yes" answer to the prayer I offered the night that I completed my study that compared the Six Pillars of Character with the Bible. I had told Him that I could not live by His standards in my own strength and asked Him to give me His strength to have genuine godly char-acter throughout this year.

Thank You, hF, for saying yes to my prayer in a way that far exceeded any of my expectations. Today You made Ephesians 3:20-21 a reality in my life. In Your name I pray, amen.

Tonight Bethany and I met for a final time together for a while. She leaves for China the day after my graduation. She, along with other Home Economics-Family and Consumer Science students and a professor, will spend the summer ministering to children. They will use their knowledge and skills in several ways. Each morning they will work in a local orphanage and/or residential school for disabled children, assisting with feeding and basic care. Afternoons will be filled with designing and presenting nutrition plans to workers in the schools or in individual homes. Of course, they will also share their faith with those to whom they minister. What an exciting way to use one's education to glorify God. I can hardly wait to be a part of a team.

This summer I will work more hours as Mom's administrative assistant, help with the younger women at New Hope Community, deepen my walk with the Lord, have fun, and prepare for college. I look forward to being on the same campus with Bethany in the fall.

As we began our time together, she reminded me why she was holding a sign that simply read REWARDED, PROVERBS 31:31 at the awards assembly. The statement represented the fruit of my having sought to cultivate the 11 principles of Proverbs 31:10–31 that we wanted to apply to our lives throughout the year. Just as the godly woman receives her rewards "in the gates," which refers the public assembly of people, so the Lord allowed me to be rewarded in my public assembly, West Ranch High. The godly woman does not have to brag about herself but, rather, is praised by those who know her best. In my case it was my peers, teachers, and staff of the school. (Quite honestly, I never visualized myself as the recipient of the award.) Bethany said that the woman who chooses to embrace these 11 principles is usually rewarded in this life and always in the hereafter. We spent some time reviewing the principles by anticipating the potential benefits that the WTIP might anticipate if she allows her heavenly Father to mature them in her life.

Virtuous
- An intimate relationship with her heavenly Father (Matthew 5:8).
- Blessing from the Lord and righteousness from the God of her salvation (Psalm 24:1–5).
- The assurance that her influence will never die (Proverbs 31:28; 2 Timothy 1:3–7).

Trustworthy
- Those who know her best trust her. This establishes a firm foundation for her husband trusting her if she marries (Proverbs 31:11).
- An honorable reputation (Proverbs 31:25).
- The confidence that as she walks uprightly her heavenly Father will provide grace, glory, and all that is good for her (Psalm 84:11).

Energetic
- Her family benefits from her efforts (Proverbs 31:24).
- Enjoys spiritual and academic stimulation (Proverbs 27:17).
- Is exempt from reaping the fruit of slothfulness (Proverbs 19:15).

Physically Fit
- Enjoys the tasks she undertakes to their fullest potential (Colossians 3:23).
- Her body is an appropriate dwelling place for the Holy Spirit (1 Corinthians 6:19–20).
- Avoids the type of judgment and denouncement God executed on the women of Judah (Isaiah 3:16–26).

Economical
- Embraces a spiritual attitude toward money and material possessions (1 Timothy 6:6–8).
- Experiences the joy of generosity (2 Corinthians 9:6–8).
- Perceives that her purchases are good choices—no guilt (Proverbs 31:18).

Unselfish
- The joy of giving to others with the right attitude (2 Corinthians 9:7).
- Is pleasing to the Lord (Proverbs 19:17).
- Enjoys the fruit of giving to others (Acts 9:36–42).

Prepared
- Meets the design of God's plan for her life (Jeremiah 17:7–8).
- Is an authentic role model for others (1 Corinthians 11:1).
- An absence of frustration and regret in her life (Matthew 25:21, 23).

Honorable
- Her moral integrity allows her to reflect on fulfillment in later life, rather than a wasted life filled with remorse and sin (2 Corinthians 9:6; Galatians 6:7–9).
- She behaves in a way that reflects her position as a daughter of God's royal family (Genesis 1:26–27).
- A confidence that her convictions are based upon biblical principles rather than cultural trends (Psalm 119:11, 105).

Prudent
- People are willing to confide in her and trust her to retain their confidences (Proverbs 15:1–2).
- Enjoys the privilege of encouraging and affirming others (Hebrews 10:24:2–5).
- People will seek and follow her advice (Colossians 4:6).

Lovable
- Enjoys a healthy, growing, love relationship with her Lord (Matthew 22:37).
- Those closest to her love, honor, respect, and praise her (Proverbs 31:28–29).
- Lives in such a way that she is an example for the "younger women" (Titus 2:3–5).

God-fearing
- Is a positive role model because of her faith (the epistle of James in action).
- Chooses to consistently be a faithful servant (Matthew 25:21).
- Experiences the benefits of learning from the experiences of others (1 Corinthians 10).
- Realizing that her motive for cultivating these eleven principles is to glorify God (1 Corinthians 10:31), to hear her Heavenly Father say, "...well done, good and faithful servant..." (Matthew 25:21), and to cast her rewards at the feet of her

King (Revelation 4:10–11), the WTIP pursues the eternal crown with enthusiasm! As we concluded our time together we prayed for one another that we would always, regardless of our age, choose to be women who please God!

?4U

— I listed the ways that the principle of virtuous apply to this topic.
— I listed practical ways that I can apply the principle of virtuous to my life. I am praying that my heavenly Father will motivate me to put the items on the list into action.
— Using the "I Will…" portion of this chapter as a model, I wrote my commitment to becoming a young woman who pleases God.
— I supported each "I Will…" with Scripture.
— I'm asking someone to hold me accountable to fulfilling my commitment.
— I evaluated the personal goals I set for the 11 principles adopted by a Wise Teen in Progress in chapter one.
— I recorded specific examples of my growth, for example, people are willing to confide in me because I now have better control of my tongue (Prudent).
— I set new goals for increased growth towards being a WTIP.
— I reviewed each of the rewards that a WTIP could anticipate if she chooses to cultivate the 11 principles of Proverbs 31:10–31. I rewrote each anticipated reward as a question. I will use the questions to periodically measure my growth toward being a WTIP. This is my first question:

Do I have an intimate relationship with my heavenly Father (Matthew 5:8)?
— I studied the life of the widow of Zarephath (1 Kings 17:7–14) and
— Described the tasks she performed that proved she was virtuous.
— I wrote down how the tasks she completed affected her future

- I also studied the life of Mary of Bethany (John 12:1–11) and
- I described the tasks she performed that proved she was virtuous.
- I recorded how the tasks she completed affected her future.

I place all of the tools that I mentioned in this section of my journal. It's my prayer that you will use each one to mature into a Wise Teen in Progress.

CHAT — JOURNALING TIPS

Here are some journaling tips that might be helpful to you:

1. Set yourself up for success by collecting the necessary supplies. Though needs will vary for every person, some common items are:
   - Your Bible.
   - A notebook or journal. Pick one that invites you to write in it.
   - Your copy of <u>Becoming a Young Woman Who Pleases God</u>.
   - A supply of pencils, pens, and other tools like a highlighter. It's handy to store them in a zipper pouch.
   - Index cards for verses to memorize and mediate upon. You may also want a notebook ring to keep the cards together.
   - Sticky notes for reminders (especially for thoughts that distract your mind while you are journaling. Write them down so that you won't forget them. This will discourage Satan from sidetracking you).
   - A basket, box, or other container to store your supplies.

2. Begin your journaling time by asking your heavenly Father to help you accurately record your thoughts. Don't be in a hurry to begin writing.
3. You might want to write some verses to begin your journal as I did in chapter 1.
4. After you pray, record the thoughts that are important to you.

WTIP Tools

5. Consider closing your journal entries by writing a prayer to your heavenly Father as I did.
6. Weekly read your journal entries. I found that my love for my heavenly Father and others grows as I review them.
7. Consider writing your responses to MAKING THE CHAPTER PRACTICAL in either your journal or another notebook. These activities are ways that I personally applied biblical truth to daily life.
8. Read the Scriptures that I referred to in my entries. I purposely didn't write them in my journal so that I read and study them in my Bible when I review the entries.
9. Divide the MAKING THE CHAPTER PRACTICAL activities into small parts. I am able to remember and apply more of what I study to my life when I don't read or write too much at one time.
10. Memorize and meditate upon some of the verses you study. Psalm 119:11 teaches us that hiding God's Word in our hearts is the most effective weapon to prevent us from sinning.
11. Read the verses from your Bible.
12. Write the ones you want to memorize and meditate upon on one of your index cards. If you are artistic you might enjoy decorating it at another time. I created a sample card for your below.

"For the LORD GOD is a sun and shield;
The LORD gives grace and glory;
No good thing does He withhold
from those who walk uprightly."
Psalm 84:11

(front)

09/12—Father, you know how diligently I studied for the English test today. I know others cheated. Help me to believe that You will not withhold the academic honors I desire to receive for Your glory.

(back)

13. Put the card in a place where you often see it. This helps you to think about your heavenly Father's special instructions to you.
14. Record each time you use the verse to help you to say no to sin. Write the situation and the results on the back of the card (2 Corinthians 10:3–6; Ephesians 6:17; Hebrews 4:12).
15. Meditate (continually think) upon the Scriptures and your comments often. Remember that meditating helps you to focus on your heavenly Father's faithfulness to you.

It was my joy to share with you some of tips I used to record the events that shaped my character during my senior year in high school. I now look forward to journaling my college experiences (this time I may even buy my own journal). I pray that you are excited about the wonderful things God has planned for you in the next season of your life. Let's partner together to always choose to be young women who please God (Ecclesiastes 4:9–12)!

In His Love,
Sarah Joy
Philippians 1:6

CULTIVATING A HEART OF GRATITUDE

God's Word teaches us to cultivate a thankful, encouraging spirit! This project is designed to help you to focus on cultivating a heart of gratitude.

Read Chapter 5 in Becoming a Woman Who Pleases God. Create a bulleted list of the concepts learned.

Simple things I am thankful for:

Specific people I am thankful for:

Write a note of gratitude to at least five of the names you listed. Place a check mark by their names when the notes have been sent.

My reaction to Expressing Gratitude:

Evaluate your Gratitude Gauge Score.

Use the verses that follow to develop principles for increasing your Gratitude Gauge Score. Several examples are provided for you.

- Psalm 18:49—I will choose to give thanks to God and sing praises to His name.
- Psalm 103:3-5—I am to recall all of God's benefits to me:
- Forgiveness of sin (103:3).
- Recovery from sickness (103:3).
- Deliverance from death (103:4).
- Abundant lovingkindness and mercy (103:4).
- Food to sustain life (103: 5).
- Romans 1:21—Thankless is a trait of unbelievers.
- 1 Thessalonians 5:18—It's God's will for me to give thanks in everything.

What will you do with the truth you learned?

Scripture Menu

CULTIVATING A HEART OF GRATITUDE

Verses for Principle Development

1. 2 Samuel 22:50
2. 1 Chronicles 16:4
3. 1 Chronicles 16:7
4. 1 Chronicles 16:34
5. 1 Chronicles 16:35
6. 1 Chronicles 16:41
7. 1 Chronicles 23:30
8. 2 Chronicles 31:2
9. 1 Chronicles 29:6–14
10. Ezra 3:11
11. Psalm 6:5
12. Psalm 18:49
13. Psalm 30:4
14. Psalm 30:12
15. Psalm 35:18
16. Psalm 50:14
17. Psalm 69:30
18. Psalm 75:1
19. Psalm 79:13
20. Psalm 92:1
21. Psalm 95:2
22. Psalm 97:12
23. Psalm 100:4
24. Psalm 105:1
25. Psalm 106:1
26. Psalm 106:47
27. Psalm 107:1
28. Psalm 116:17
29. Psalm 118:1–29
30. Psalm 119:62
31. Psalm 136:1–26
32. Psalm 140:13
33. Daniel 2:23–6:10
34. Matthew 11:25
35. Matthew 26:27
36. Mark 8:6
37. Mark 14:23
38. Luke 2:38
39. Luke 17:16
40. Luke 22:17–19
41. John 6:11–23
42. Acts 27:35
43. Romans 1:8
44. Romans 1:21
45. Romans 6:17
46. Romans 7:23–25
47. 1 Corinthians 1:4
48. 1 Corinthians 11:24
49. 1 Corinthians 15:57
50. 2 Corinthians 1:11
51. 2 Corinthians 2:14
52. 2 Corinthians 9:11
53. 2 Corinthians 9:15
54. Ephesians 1:16
55. Ephesians 5:4
56. Ephesians 5:20
57. Philippians 1:3
58. Philippians 4:6
59. Colossians 1:3
60. Colossians 1:12
61. Colossians 2:7
62. Colossians 3:15–17
63. Colossians 4:2
64. 1 Thessalonians 1:2
65. 1 Thessalonians 3:9
66. 1 Thessalonians 5:18
67. 2 Thessalonians 1:3
68. 1 Timothy 1:12
69. 1 Timothy 2:1
70. 1 Timothy 4:4
71. 2 Timothy 1:3
72. Philemon 1:4
73. Hebrews 13:15
74. Revelation 4:9
75. Verse of own choice

BUILDING MY BUDGET

Use the form below or develop your own to record your weekly income and expenses.

CATEGORY	AMOUNT
Income$	
Allowance	
Salary	
Gifts	
Loans	
Total Income =	$
Fixed Expenses	$
Tithing	
Car insurance	
Gas	
Total Fixed Expenses =	$
Variable Expenses	$
School supplies	
My portion of my clothing budget	
Entertainment	
Gifts	
Total Variable Expenses =	$
Savings	$
An established percentage	
of each paycheck	
Total Savings =	$
Grand Total =	$

Once you have used the chart for several weeks, revise it, if necessary, to best meet your personal goals.

Word Up—THE IDEAL MAN

Develop guidelines for the selection of a Christian boyfriend by responding to the statements below. The response should utilize Scripture that has been written in question form. A minimum of five Scriptures should be selected for each category.

1. This man places God's business above any of his own affairs.
   a. Matthew 6:33—Does this man consistently seek God's kingdom first?
   b.
   c.
   d.
   e.
   f.

2. This man teaches and sets a good example.
   a. Philippians 3:17—Can this man say, "be followers together of me?"
   b.
   c.
   d.
   e.
   f.

3. This man recognizes that anyone who needs him is his neighbor.
   a. Luke 10:27—Does he love his neighbor as himself?
   b.
   c.
   d.
   e.
   f.

4. This man measures his giving by what he has left rather than what he gives.
   a. 2 Corinthians 9:6—Does this man sow bountifully or sparingly?
   b.
   c.
   d.
   e.
   f.

5. This man reads God's word consistently and eagerly.
   a. 2 Timothy 2:15—Does this man study to show himself approved unto God?
   b.
   c.
   d.

e.

f.

6. This man lays up treasures in heaven rather than pleasures on earth.

a. Matthew 6:20, 21—where is this man storing his treasure?

b.

c.

d.

e.

f.

7. This man has his priorities in the right order (Lord, family, schoolwork, girlfriend).

a. Matthew 22:37—Does this man love his Lord with all his heart, mind, and soul?

b.

c.

d.

e.

f.

8. This man sees his own faults before he sees the faults of others.

a. Matthew 7:3—Does this man consider the beam that is in his own eye?

b.

c.

d.

e.

f.

9. This man desires to help others rather than serve himself.

a. Philippians 2:3,4—Does this man esteem others better than himself?

b.

c.

d.

e.

f.

10. Does this man recognize that all of his life should be lived distinctively?

a. 1 Corinthians 10:31—Do his actions bring glory to God?

b.

c.

d.

e.

f.

Books

C. J. Mahaney, *The Soul of Modesty* (Audio) (Little Rock: Family Life Today, 2003).

Charles Hummel, T*yranny of the Urgent* (Downers Grove, IL: InterVarsity, 1967).

Dannah Gresh, *Secret Keeper Girl: 8 Great Dates for You and Your Daughter* with CD (Audio) (Chicago: Moody Publishers, 2004).

Since my mom teaches younger women how to practice the Titus 2 principles in their lives, works in New Hope's Women's Ministries, and is a published author, she knows lots of helpful resources for ladies. I asked her to prepare a list to put in my notebook so I also help my friends share God's special instructions for women with their moms.

Donna Morley, *Becoming a Woman of Spiritual Passion* (Eugene: Harvest House Publishers, 2005).

Edith Schaeffer, *The Hidden Art of Homemaking* (Wheaton: Tyndale House, 1985).

Elizabeth George, *A Woman After God's Own Heart* (Eugene: Harvest House Publishers, 2006).

Elizabeth Prentiss, *Stepping Heavenward* (Uhrichsville: Barbour Publishing, Inc., 1998).

Glynnis Whitwer, *Work @ Home: A Practical Guide for Women Who Want to Work from Home* (Birmingham: New Hope Publishers, 2007).

Ingrid Schlueter, "It's 911 Time for Christian Girlhood" (2007). Found at http://www.christianworldviewnetwork.com/article.php/1503/Ingrid_Schlueter.

John MacArthur, *Think Biblically! Recovering a Christian Worldview* (Chicago: Crossway Books, 2003).

John MacArthur, *Whose Money Is It Anyway?* (Nashville: Word Publishing, 2000).

John Piper and Wayne Grudem, *Recovering Biblical Manhood & Womanhood* (Wheaton: Crossway Books, 2006).

Karen Ehman, *A Life That Says Welcome* (Grand Rapids: Revell, 2006).

Karen Ehman, *The Complete Guide to Getting & Staying Organized* (Eugene: Harvest House Publishers, 2008).

Lydia Brownback, *Legacy of Faith: From Women of the Bible to Women of Today* (Phillipsburg: P&R Publishing, 2002).

Martha Peace, *Becoming a Titus 2 Woman* (Bemidji: Focus Publishing, Inc., 1997).

Mary Hunt, *Debt-Proof Living* (Los Angeles: DPL Press, 2005).

Mary Hunt, *Live Your Life for Half the Price* (Los Angeles: DPL Press, 2005).

Nancy Leigh DeMoss, *Choosing Forgiveness: Your Journey to Freedom* (Chicago: Moody Press, 2006).

Nancy Leigh DeMoss, *Lies Women Believe and The Truth That Sets Them Free* (Chicago: Moody Press, 2001).

Nancy Leigh DeMoss, *The Look: Does God Really Care What I Wear?* (Buchanan: Revive Our Hearts, 2003).

Nancy Leigh DeMoss, *Modesty: Does God Really Care What I Wear?* (Audio) (Buchanan: Revive Our Hearts, 2003).

Pat Ennis, *Precious in His Sight: The Fine Art of Becoming a Godly Woman* (Sisters: Trustedbooks, 2006).

Pat Ennis and Lisa Tatlock, *Designing a Lifestyle That Pleases God: A Practical Guide* (Chicago: Moody, 2004).

Pat Ennis and Lisa Tatlock, *Becoming a Woman Who Pleases God: A Guide to Developing Your Biblical Potential* (Chicago: Moody, 2003).

Pat Ennis and Lisa Tatlock, *Practicing Hospitality: the Joy of Serving Others* (Wheaton: Crossway, 2007).

Sites
www.biblegateway.com
www.crosswalk.com
www.charactercounts.org
www.newhopepublishers.com
www.saltinstitute.org
www.americanheartassociation.org
www.experian.com
www.worldcraftsvillage.com

Sites
I hope you enjoyed meeting the people in <u>Becoming a Young Woman Who Pleases God</u>. Each one had a twenty-first-century message to communicate. As well, they all were selected from the pages of Scripture. The chart below matches each person with his or her biblical counterpart. Spend time studying the life of each. As you conclude learning about each person, ask yourself the question, "how did the study of this person affect my life?"

<u>People You Met</u>	<u>Biblical Counterpart</u>
Sarah Joy Abramson	Sarah
Zach Abramson	Zachariah
Liz Abramson	Elizabeth
Mr. Solomon	Solomon (study Proverbs & Ecclesiastes)
Pastor John	John the Baptist
Bethany	Mary of Bethany
Bekka	Young Rebecca
	Mature Rebecca
Abigail	Abigail
David	David
Timothy	Timothy
Mrs. Titus (Mrs. T.)	The Titus 2 Woman

New Hope® Publishers is a division of WMU®, an international organization that challenges Christian believers to understand and be radically involved in God's mission. For more information about WMU, go to www.wmu.com. More information about New Hope books may be found at www.newhopepublishers.com. New Hope books may be purchased at your local bookstore.

If you've been blessed by this book, we would like to hear your story. We welcome your comments and suggestions at: newhopereader@wmu.org, Check us out online too.

Other Teen Devotionals from

New Hope

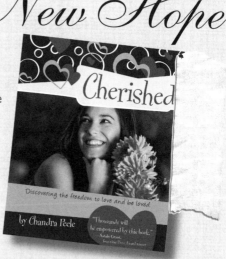

Cherished
Discovering the Freedom to Love
and Be Loved
Chandra Peele
ISBN-10: 1-59669-250-2
ISBN-13: 978-1-59669-250-3

Crash Course
Forming a Faith Foundation for Life
Daniel Darling
ISBN-10: 1-59669-285-5
ISBN-13: 978-1-59669-285-5

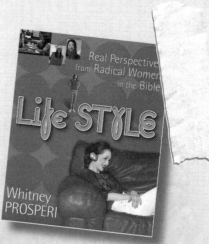

LifeSTYLE
Real Perspectives from
Radical Women in the Bible
Whitney Prosperi
ISBN-10: 1-56309-812-1
ISBN-13: 978-1-56309-812-3

Available in bookstores
everywhere.

NEW HOPE
P U B L I S H E R S

For information about these books or any New Hope product.
visit www.newhopepublishers.com.